The Culture of Vanlife

There's real life for you, embodied in that little cart. The open road, the dusty highway, the heath, the common, villages, towns, cities! Here today, up and off to somewhere else tomorrow! travel, change, interest, excitement! the whole world before you, and a horizon that's always changing!

- Mr Toad in *Wind in the Willows,* Kenneth Grahame

The Lucky Vanlife
HN LT 28H

The Rolling Home presents

THE CULTURE OF VANLIFE

LANNOO

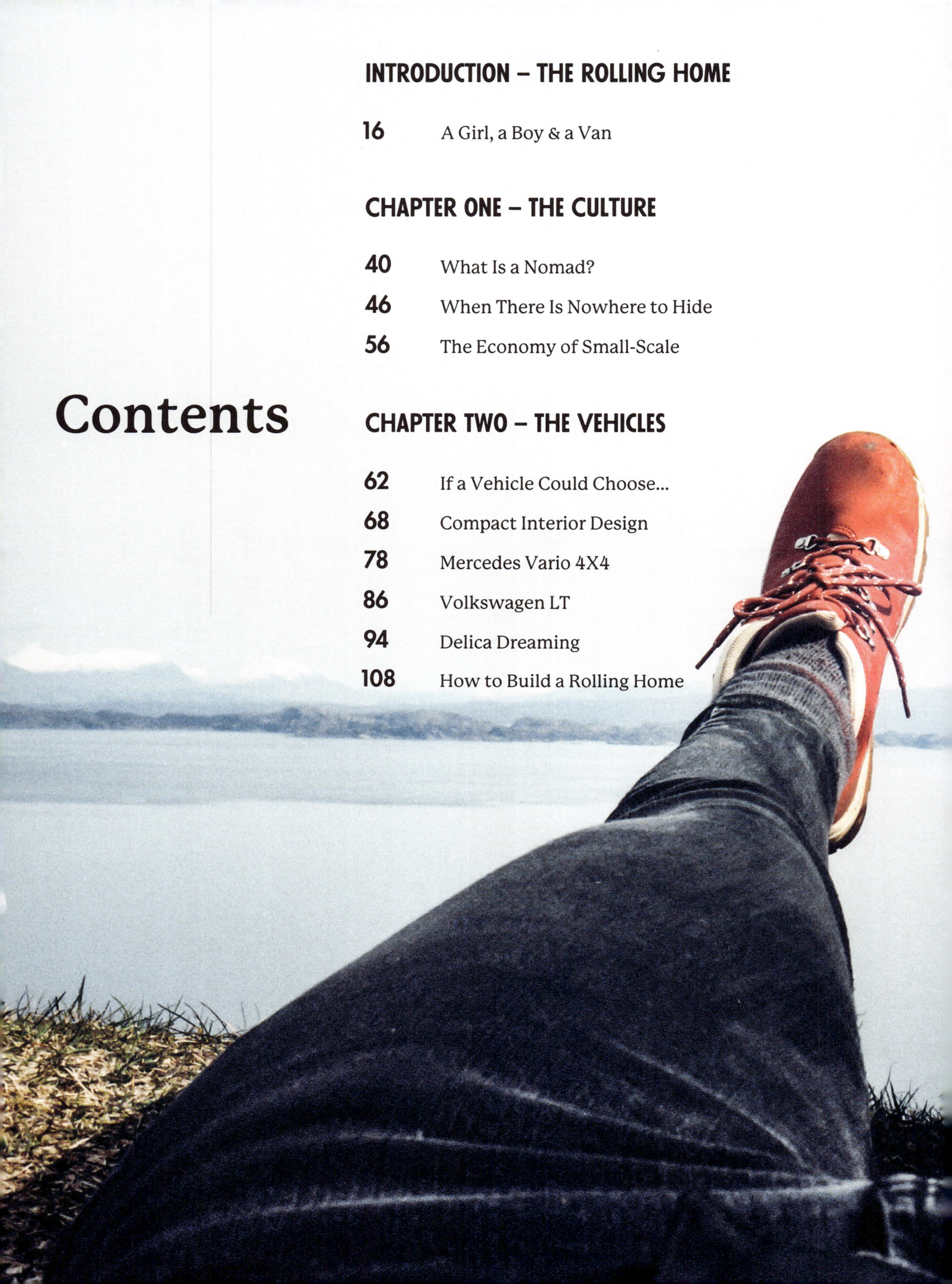

Contents

CHAPTER THREE – THE PEOPLE

CHAPTER FOUR – THE PLACES

CHAPTER FIVE – THE FUTURE

Introduction

THE ROLLING HOME STORY

A Girl, a Boy & a Van

by Calum Creasey and Lauren Smith

I have a lot of conversations about camper vans. It is true that they fill my day in many ways. Vehicles that usually consist of a bed, a place to cook or prepare food and a spot to sit comfortably out of the rain. I see a converted van drive past me on the street and sometimes name the make and model. I pass a van similar to ours here in Cornwall and can't help but wave. Parked on clifftops, by beaches or in supermarket car parks. We all come across camper vans in our daily lives – the types of vehicles that have been adapted for human beings to live in. Altered so that we can feel comfort far from home. Sometimes built to be our only home. These are the vehicles that fill my conversations and this book.

Our van is a 1996 Volkswagen Transporter and it has a lot to answer for. In many ways it has dictated the passage of our life to this point. I am certain that this was not its purpose when it rolled out of the factory in Germany, a short-wheelbase, relatively underpowered panel van. A large steel box with a four-cylinder diesel engine. Its first trip was to the UK when it was registered by an engineering firm. Following 14 years of hard graft, our van got its first real break. In 2010 I purchased it to replace my earlier, self-built Nissan Vanette. In the act of adding simple pine furniture, carpeted walls, a gas burner and a porthole window, we created what we now call 'the Rolling Home'. Like most of the self-converted camper vans we see, ours was not initially designed to be lived in. Yet we changed that and in doing so changed our lives for the better. It is a modest story and one that has played out for many people across Europe and the world. We take these often old and beat-up vehicles and turn them into something else – catalysts for happiness.

HOME
SWEET
ROLLING
HOME

The van in question might be huge and have seats for all the family, or it might be small with only space for two. A blow-up mattress and a camping stove might suffice. Trips that may be dictated by the span of the weekend, or else that ferry ticket may be for a one-way voyage. What all of our van stories share is in essence the act of searching and often finding that which is elusive in our lives. Since we have owned our van, we too have searched.

As teenagers we built it. As young adults we packed it for trips outside our parents' houses. As a couple, our van became the vessel that housed our love of life and of each other. Open the sliding door and that love would pour out. Onto beaches and clifftops. It would wrap around us and our friends and mingle with bonfire smoke and laughter. You can see it in the photos and on the faces of all of us. Etched in happiness. When it was time to move on, those feelings would fly with us back to the van and fill all of the gaps between ourselves and the vehicle.

When we returned and tried other ways of living, renting a chocolate-box English cottage not far from where we grew up, trying out office jobs and careers we may have been destined for, nothing ever felt as real as that van. It always represented something that we could so easily reach out to and embrace. Like the empty suitcase at the back of the wardrobe, only far more alluring. When you are faced with bills and rent, it still sits there. Even driving it as a daily vehicle can be a torturous affair, always feeling the pull towards the sea or the ferry port.

Until again you find yourself fully seduced. With the turn of a key, normal life gives way to nervousness, fear, trepidation and, ultimately, happiness. We wanted all of those things to come in torrents, we wanted them to surround us and envelop our very being, we wanted to feel truly alive. When all that you own surrounds you in a small camper van, this happens without you even knowing.

This is the story of 'the Rolling Home', of how a simple vehicle and a simple idea can hold so much power. Since those early trips we have spent a great deal of time trying to get back to how it felt. What we learned as young adults – lessons of simplicity and the importance of travel, translated into a life that we felt we had built for ourselves. To this day I feel indebted to that vehicle. Protective even, so that when it breaks down I feel quite emotional. It is no longer our full-time home: it now feels like an old friend. One that has shared life's ups and downs with us, but is always willing to head off into the unknown, no questions asked.

So the tale goes that we travelled tens of thousands of miles throughout Europe on many trips between 2010 and 2017. In 2016 we self-published a photographic book that was supported by wonderful people through crowdfunding. Since then 'the Rolling Home' has become a byword for the vanlife movement on social media, giving us an incredible opportunity to launch further creative projects and spread the word on just how life-changing owning a camper van can be. In the years that followed the crowdfunding campaign, we bounced from our home town to a friend's farm then back to Europe, and eventually set up home by the sea in Cornwall, UK. Now I spread my time between a small workshop, where we build camper vans, and compiling a magazine celebrating alternative living, the *Rolling Home Journal.*

Sure, travelling in a van sometimes means no showers for a few days, oily hands and serious dents in your bank account, but you'll have smiles on your faces none the less. Owning a camper van may be one of the best ways to hold on to a romantic outlook on this sometimes unromantic life. We can count ourselves as part of an international movement that has come to be known as vanlife. A shared passion for camper vans, a huge online community, a gathering of like-minded people. Vanlife is all of these things and more. I think culture is created when people from different places discover that they share ideas. Their dreams are somewhat aligned and their lifestyles are similar in many ways. In this book we explore the culture of vanlife through some of the ideas and people that make it so wonderful.

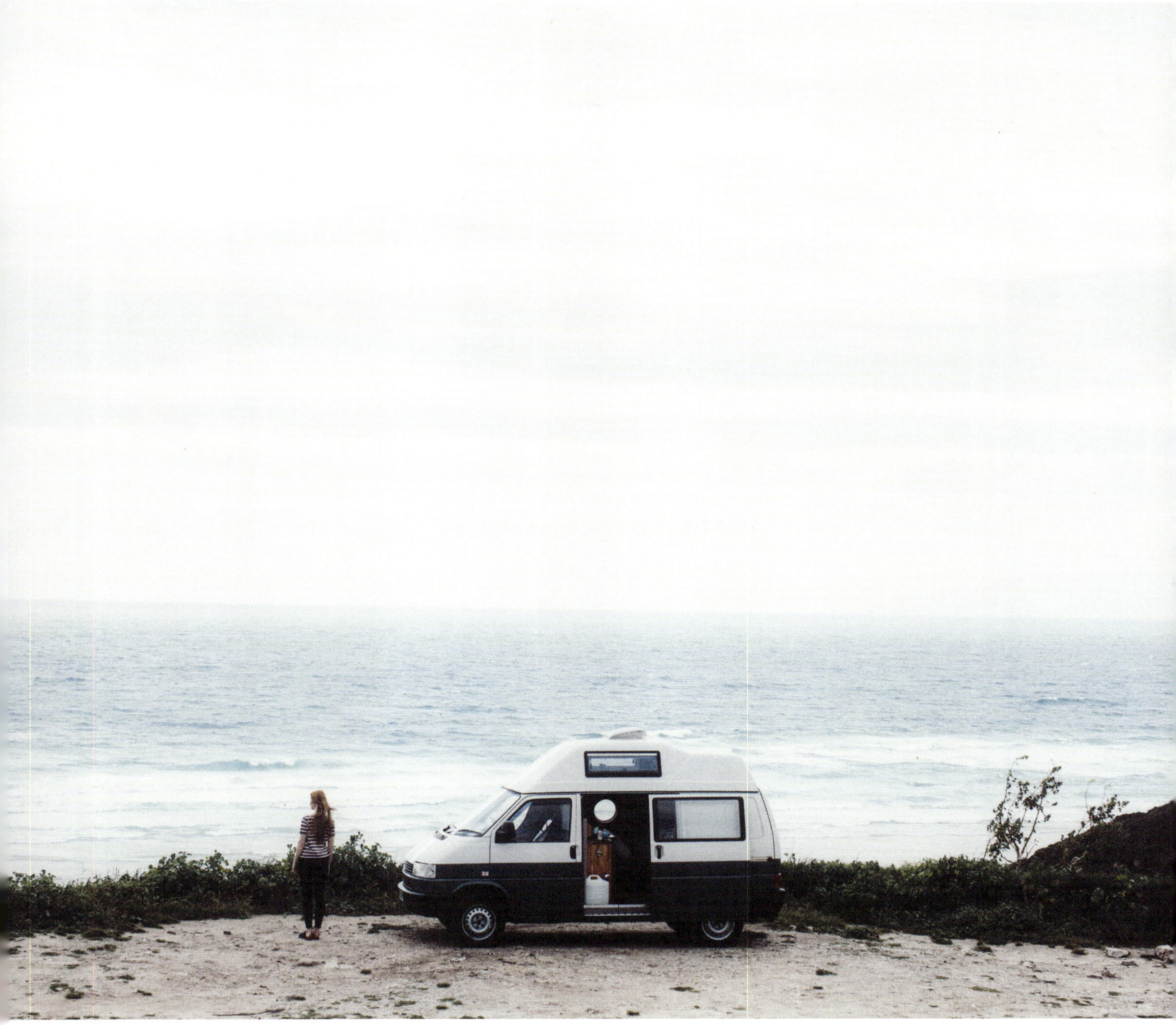

ROCHE
PAYS D'OC
2014

N207 BVV

Ektar 100
POWER GAS
PROPANE/ISOBUTANE
230 G/8.1 OZ
SILVA

Carre

Chapter one

THE CULTURE

What Is a Nomad?

by Dan Crockett

Essay exploring the human definition of 'the nomad'

Answer: 'A person who does not stay long in the same place, a wanderer.'

'For all its material advantages, the sedentary life has left us edgy, unfulfilled. Even after 400 generations in villages and cities, we haven't forgotten. The open road still softly calls, like a nearly forgotten song of childhood.'
Carl Sagan, *Pale Blue Dot*

To wander is an almost universal human desire. Far back in our heritage, early *Homo sapiens* simply stood up and turned its back on the warmth and security of permanent shelter to seek new horizons. Why? For practical reasons (climate or food supply or human threat), we have always survived by searching for new lands. But we still do not really understand the craving at the heart of the human spirit, that basic restlessness to go beyond the horizon.

In *Pale Blue Dot*, Carl Sagan quotes Herman Melville: 'I am tormented with an everlasting itch for things remote.' Until only very recently, human beings were a nomadic species. Some still are: Australian aborigines, Sami reindeer herders in Scandinavia, the Romany people, Mongolian nomads – history is full of rich, diverse nomadic cultures, almost all of which have been impacted by the modern world. A full list would more than overflow this book. But without romanticizing or objectifying this existence, can parallels be drawn between historic and contemporary nomads? Are we all at heart nomadic? Has this instinct been suppressed by a motionless, modern existence? When we sit at our screens seeking escape, are our dreams of freedom entwined with this basic genetic urge? Can parallels therefore be drawn between contemporary alternative living and those human beings who have always searched? On a lonely, forgotten highway, are we running away from or going in search of what we really are? This essay traces nomads from prehistory to the present, explores the roots of our desire for freedom, and guesses at where this movement might lead.

What we are

'The more high-tech we become, the more nature we need.'
Richard Louv

When Charles Darwin published *On the Origin of Species* and his theory of natural selection in 1859, it was incredibly controversial. The Victorian public of the day – and indeed many people to the present day who believe in creationism – was outraged by Darwin's claims that humanity descended from animals. As well as calling into question the dominant idea of the time, that God made each species and man in his own image, it removed man from a fiercely guarded pedestal. Writing a little later, the poet Rilke said:

And only then, when I have learned enough,
I will go to watch the animals, and let
Something of their composure slowly glide
Into my limbs; will see my own existence deep within their eyes.

Darwin's theory paved the way for genetics and evolutionary thought. It ties us back to the molecules that assembled into organisms 3.8 billion years ago. It also ties us back to the *Homo sapiens* that left its East African homeland 70,000 years ago and started to settle in Europe and Asia. These were our nomad ancestors. Physically and mentally they were very similar to us, even if the world they lived in and the way they interpreted it was anything but.

But what we are has not changed. Animals surrounded by a vastly complex and fascinating habitat, the world all around us. That world may be reduced, its biodiversity collapsing and natural spaces shrinking rapidly, but as sensory beings that evolved to experience it, we remain largely the same entity.

The present

'Humankind, after all, cannot bear very much reality.'
Robert Pogue Harrison

'Technology is not merely augmenting but replacing real human contact.'
Paul Shepard

If we leap to the present day, the world we occupy is understood through objects. Everything we do, from eating breakfast to travelling to work, takes place through a complex grid of invented devices. These may be functional (shoes), pleasurable (music) or simply unavoidable (tax). Over the course of a lifetime we will, usually very briefly, own millions of objects. Our default modes of existence encourage us to accumulate. We buy or build repositories to store all this stuff – fridges, houses, cupboards. In *Branded Nation*, James Twitchell posits, 'Much of our shared knowledge about ourselves and our culture comes to us through a commercial process of storytelling called branding ... Ten percent of a two year old's nouns are brand names.' The fireside story has been replaced with the digitally delivered advertisement. It is powerfully effective, undeniably, but it is also widely appreciated that this does not make us happy. Part of the contemporary desire to wander is the lurking knowledge of this simple fact. We seek to throw off the shackles of materialism, seeking freedom from systems and structures that we didn't particularly want in the first place. At the heart of this is a wish for connection.

We are hyper-connected. Whereas our ancestors could only maintain relationships with small groups, quickly reverting to warfare or chaos when this capacity was exceeded, digital technology affords us the opportunity to monitor and interact with thousands of people every day. We watch our 'friends' or networks, many of whom we have never met or haven't seen for decades, play out their lives in a public forum. Through this medium we hope and long for a connection that largely goes unanswered. In many ways our generation and the one following are the guinea pigs for this social experiment on a massive scale. Its repercussions on our lives are as yet not understood and are only beginning to be studied. What is obvious is a groundswell of earnest desire for a simpler, more wholesome life. This is manifested, or indeed curated, on social media. Presented for a willing audience to briefly share in an interaction that supports the idea of a life of greater freedom. The zenith of this trend is the apparently perfect lives of Instagram influencers, who attract a huge following to an idealized, utopian vision of a free life.

What would the nomads of past times make of this extraordinary phenomenon? I expect they would be as addicted as we are. Technology has become the ultimate abstraction. Awareness hurts so we seek eternal distraction. We are enthralled enough to forget intimacy forever. Our connectivity has never been broader, yet something inside us has grown narrower. We can maintain a thousand remote relationships but we feel lonely. Even as a global roar engulfs us, our local surroundings become invisible. Human noise in all its diversity leaves us enchanted, drowning out every other voice. Oral culture, essential in knowing our place in the world, has been overwritten. Our myths are delivered at warp speed, holding our attention for a few minutes at most. Spellbound, our dominant sense becomes the touch of fingers upon screens. As David Abram says, 'we seal ourselves into a numbing solitude'. It is a cold, hollow feeling. Humans are shaped by the world and particularly the culture they are born into. As Mark Rowlands states: 'Humans are the animals that believe the stories they tell about themselves.' That is why some believe fervently in the Holy Ghost, others in the spirit of rocks and rivers, still more in the deity of celebrities who are famous for absolutely no reason at all. It is entirely possible to operate in the modern world without any intimacy– technology robs us of the ability to really feel anything. 'We subliminally lurch', Spencer Wells states, 'from one unrelated (and usually unwanted) stimulus to the next'. Thus we spend the majority of our time watching digital waterfalls, forgetting entirely what it feels like for cold, wild water to touch our skins. Somewhat like voyeurs in the grip of a pornography addiction, we chase digital renderings of Norwegian fjords or endless French beaches at sunset. Gradually, we are replacing the true knowledge of these interactions with a facsimile, whereby documenting the experience is more important than having the experience. Even the intention to capture changes how we process an experience completely. All of this throws us off from living in the present moment. The earnest goal of becoming more nomadic, surely, is to appreciate the present and not always dwell in an imagined future of job promotions, savings and a far-off retirement.

Where we've been

'I like to think of landscape not as a fixed place but as a path that is unwinding before my eyes, under my feet. To see and know a place is a contemplative act. It means emptying our minds and letting what is there, in all its multiplicity and endless variety, come in.'
Gretel Ehrlich

Hunter-gatherers of times past understood their environment in a completely different way. Their bodies and minds were connected to the natural environment on which they depended. There is no particular reason to romanticize or idealize this, which seems to be a common pitfall for many alternative thinkers. However, it is undeniable that time spent in non-human environments can provide a sense of security and connection that may be unavailable elsewhere. As humans rapidly become further removed from nature, they evolve to forget all about it. What this could lead to is a rootless civilization, unsure what it is exactly, struggling even more than its forebears to relate to a changing and changed world.

If they based our millions of years of evolutionary progress on the average public-transport carriage in the developed world, our ancestors would likely be puzzled. Everyone sits hunched and silent, staring down at their palms, completely immersed in worlds of their fabrication. Often what they gaze at are vestiges of a rapidly diminishing natural world – forests, mountains, animals, oceans. Thus nature in its changed form still influences our lives. It is no wonder that many seek to rebel and to go out and experience the world as it was.

The nuclear family has evolved as a human living system for simple reasons. We are economically more valuable if we stay in one place and buy things. We are less likely to become anarchists and to destabilize the whole if we are in service to a small group of family and friends. We are also less likely to kill each other and to threaten our surrounding community if we feel part of something. The issue is that this hyperindividualistic model of living shuts us off from the global community (everything beyond humans) and encourages us to prioritize our own micro dramas (relationship, job, money) above everything else. Thus shut off from the world, we forget it. The recent rise in awareness of and interest in alternative living is a response to this trend. Because so much of our society is built around trying to acquire permanence in what is ultimately a brief and transitory experience, rejecting the physical ties of a conventional life is a good place to start. Some might see this as running away or shirking responsibility. Others see it as a necessary counterpoint to a life they really do not want.

Where we're going

So what is a contemporary nomad? There are scant pockets of nomadic peoples still scattered around the world, living as they have always done. As Yuval Noah Harari says in *Sapiens*, 'on the whole foragers seemed to have enjoyed a more comfortable and rewarding lifestyle than most of the peasants, shepherds, labourers and office clerks who followed in their footsteps'. While historical wanderers travelled by foot, living off the land and using their wits to survive in a hostile natural environment, the modern nomad might travel on four wheels or two. They might create a temporary structure in a forest or on a shore, dwelling for a time to understand and map an environment. They are sensory creatures, recognizing the unquantifiable power of interaction with nature. 'Walking in the woods, lying on the grass, taking a bath in the sea, are from the outside; entering the unconscious, entering yourself through dreams, is touching nature from the inside and this is the same thing, things are put right again', Carl Jung said. E.O. Wilson found that a 'culture creates its present and therefore its future through the stories its people tell, the stories they believe, and the stories that underlie their actions. The more consistent a culture's core stories are with biological and physical reality, the more likely its people are to live in a way compatible with ecological rules and thereby persist'.

Our attempts to wrestle with digital technology, to use it to enable a better connection with the natural world as it slips away represents an authentic desire. 'Instead of intelligent, participatory relationships with our encompassing earth, we are immersed in communications reflecting humanity back to ourselves, like a hall of mirrors', Rust and Totton wrote. This is what we are seeking to transcend. The nascent movement represented in the coming pages, the exploration of new ways of living through moving, building and play, is an attempt to tell a new and better cultural story. At the heart of this new story is freedom. Its ultimate success and ability to permeate and influence the wider culture are yet to be fully understood.

When There Is Nowhere to Hide

by Mattias Wieles

A journey into vanlife and minimalism

Vanlife and minimalism, popular buzzwords of recent years. Ultimate clichés, surrounded by sometimes hollow rhetoric and often staged romanticism. It is not hard to understand that 'vanlife' and minimalism are often believed to only be a trend. Subject to temporary fashion and social-media algorithm changes. Another hashtag in the realm of the hipster lifestyle and the 'influencer' business. As is the case with many of these movements, they have built their exponential growth on the fundaments of a seemingly groundbreaking idea. One that preceded the mass interest it now receives. A countermovement that offers an opt-out from the popular way of life often starts with only a simple message. One that really touches on a primal understanding of human life. It is an ambivalent thing. These ideas that offer alternatives and escapes from mega-industries and economical strangleholds become commercial industries themselves.

Our only mission is to see through all the fuzz, to break through the stronghold and get back to the core of it all. Back to the power of an idea that at one point underpinned this whole movement. In my experience, a very effective way to reach that goal is to physically experience these concepts in real life. Let me share with you what our year-long journey taught us about these hashtags that go hand in hand so well: vanlife and minimalism.

edp
edp

Changing lifestyles

About a year ago, we drove off for an adventure of a lifetime. Two blonde millennials for a year in a little yellow van. Into unknown territory and bound by nothing and nobody. While the journey itself was a life-changing experience, the lead-up to it was a key component in learning about vanlife and minimalism. Fundamental changes don't come overnight, and discovering a new lifestyle is something that can occur unnoticed. Like a new love or friendship, that seemingly pops up out of nowhere, but has in fact been growing roots beneath the surface of everyday life. For us it was the same with vanlife. At first we just chased this dream of living and travelling in a camper van, but soon enough it started to impact our whole being. This process can be seen throughout Instagram on ample accounts, and most often comes with these typical pictures: a couple, their new (old) van, a flea market of some sort, and all their stuff up front. Accompanied by a cardboard sign: 'Going off on an adventure – everything for sale'. It almost turns the sale of all the old crap into a fundraiser for a good cause. The cause: alternative living.

We weren't any different and did precisely that. We bought an old van. A Renault Trafic, four-wheel drive. Age: too old. While our lives seemingly continued as before, our minds were wandering off already. Slowly, everything started to evolve around this one dream, to leave it all behind and be free. The practicalities of this dream, however, had an even bigger impact than the dream itself. We were still in the process of finishing our studies, and had no money and an apartment full of stuff that all of a sudden felt like a major burden. It is only in hindsight that I know that this was where minimalism quietly made its way into our lives. This was the start of our first minimalistic chapter. We sold everything, threw out all financial burdens, cut all redundancies out of our lives. All our possessions fitted in our little van now; ties had been cut, jobs left behind, subscriptions to magazines and the gym cancelled. We said our goodbyes and felt free as never before. But it was only the start; changes happened mainly on the surface. We had some suspicions as to what vanlife had to offer, and this concept of living in a van had introduced us to minimalism briefly. But in hindsight we had no idea what it would become to us personally. Vanlife and minimalism both require letting go of materialism, but in essence relate to something deeper. It was the start of a year that changed our perspective on what we want in life, where our ambitions lie, how we will spend our time and energy and passion.

NS-405-N

Setting off

On the surface, vanlife seems to represent adventure, and minimalism seems to be a countermovement to consumerism. Both movements, however, speak right to something more fundamental, something that goes to your bones. If it hits you, there is no going back. To really comprehend what that meant, we had to go on our year-long journey.

The first month or two, we remained within EU borders to get used to this type of travel. We headed for Portugal and Spain, countries that offer countless top-of-the-bill camper facilities. Living in a space of only a few square metres without decent sanitary facilities, privacy or luxuries feels adventurous for a little while. At some point, however, excitement makes room for irritation, unrequited needs and indeterminate feelings. You venture into an unknown world, but even more so into your unfamiliar self. You have to calibrate yourself, purely on your own needs, without distractions from a society of consumption and luxury. Remaining in these familiar countries required only a little effort and offered headspace and emotional capacity to deal with ourselves.

It was only then, after two months, that we felt in balance and ready for more. We had set out to explore the countries beyond the European borders, and so we did. In about ten months, we made our way through Morocco, Albania, Turkey and Georgia. I could write a book about the beautiful places we visited, the adventures we set out on, the fun we had. These memories will last us a long while, but the magnitude of our journey, for me, originates in something else.

The simple life

Once we had set out beyond the familiarities of Western-style civilization, things started to change for us. First of all, we entered a new level of simplicity in our own lifestyles. All of a sudden, we had to deal with water scarcity; we had to get used to buying only limited types of food in smaller shops or in the street. We had to shower even less than before, put a forced end to buying stuff at all, and stopped drinking alcohol during our Morocco travels. In other words: our lives became simpler.

Surprisingly, we now felt less special, or out of place, than we did in Spain and Portugal. Obviously we were quite the sight – two blondies in mostly Muslim countries. But at the same time we fitted in naturally. Here, everybody was driving vintage vans and cars. We weren't the only ones living the simple life. It wasn't just us living outside most of the time. The simple life was the norm rather than a deviation. The simple life has a fancy touch to it here in Western Europe, as if it's a brand. Your personal brand. In countries like Morocco, however, there is no hipster hashtag to fit the lifestyle. It is a natural state of being that needs no further exploitation or explanation.

In this simple state of being, apparent distinctions between vanlife and minimalism become irrelevant. Usually, minimalism evokes clean, empty spaces. Neat stylish houses with only a designer couch in front of a big glass window. Vanlife often comes at the other end of the spectrum. There is some style, but in practice there is a shabby character to it, which corresponds to the nomadic lifestyle. Outdated vehicles, dusty and rusty homes. Packed with items that fit the outdoor lifestyle. Just like a nomad with his donkeys and sheep, but the sheep have made room for surfboards, and the donkeys have transformed into bikes. Classy minimalism, on the one hand, and hippie vanlife, on the other. Despite their apparent differences, however, they have a lot in common. In a setting where life is simple, appearances fade, and only the core of these concepts remains.

At the crossroads of vanlife and minimalism, decluttering seems to be the mantra and consumerism is the common enemy. These are, however, only responses to flaws in Western societies. Minimalism and vanlife, however, draw strength not from protest, but from a powerful independent message about the essence of life.

From that perspective, decluttering and letting go of materialism are only routes to a deeper goal or message. But what is that message precisely?

The journey into the self

The key message will be different for every single person. The message of vanlife and minimalism is already in you. The key message is you.

While vanlife and minimalism seem catchy, offer beautiful 'content' and are very suitable for fast-paced, superficial social-media activities, in essence they are complete opposites. Social media tend to put layers and appearances and pretences between the transmitter and receiver, but vanlife and minimalism in fact attempt the contrary. Vanlife and minimalism simplify things. People who are fond of these concepts will soon enough start to eliminate noise and anything unnecessary from their lives. These concepts at the very core are the best remedy against appearances. They simplify life, and at the very simplest of life, there is no hiding. No hiding from the way things are, from who you are. If you think of yourself as both the transmitter and receiver of how you present yourself, vanlife and minimalism take away all the possible ways of not seeing yourself for who you are. There are no fancy new clothes, no cool pretentious jobs, no impressive cars, no new smartphones. All the things that seemingly offer identity only help you to forget about who you are. They offer an opt-out, a way to stay away from your true self. Vanlife and minimalism quietly eliminate all the noise between your self-image and your true self. They simplify life, and in a simple life, all that is left is you, the actual physical world around you, and your loved ones. Within that clear spectrum of what life is about, you can start calibrating your value system, you can find true passion, you can get to know yourself, and start accepting. The key message of vanlife and minimalism is you.

For us at least, this was what 11 months on the road had to offer. The mix of living simply ourselves and of venturing into cultures and lands that are prime examples of simple life was eye-opening to say the least. A simple life and poverty are often easily confused. Many families we met had challenges with water scarcity, a lack of educational opportunities, or general struggles to maintain a minimal living standard. Living simply wasn't the issue.

Ghassan, the mineworker we met in Morocco, didn't seem to be bothered by the simplicity of life. He worked tireless hours, in his seven-day work week, in an abandoned mine to be able to provide his son with decent schooling. How he lived, though, was in fact inspirational and peaceful. His personal needs made us think of the restfulness of a monk and his attitude to life seemed utterly accepting and in balance, despite his continuous struggle in the dark mines. Ghassan had nowhere to hide from himself, and because of that, was a blessing to be with. I'd rather stay with Ghassan for a while than spend time with a 'successful' banker.

Back to civilization

At some point, we had to turn around and head home. My mother had asked me before we had set off whether I was afraid of a radical change to my character. One that makes a return to society impossible. One that leaves you lost for a long time. I wasn't, but I had underestimated her assessment. The road changes you, the simple life demands a change of the self. Or, better said: a change of the self-image. I was mistaken in my assumptions about what I am. I had grown accustomed to what I tend to be, conditioned by Western society. But we deleted all the fuzz, we skipped all the noise for a year, and chose for radical calibration. We feel empowered to live an alternative lifestyle that corresponds with our own needs and lives rather than what businesses, society or standards want for us. We feel supported, not by cool brands or hashtags, but by Ghassan and the countless families and people that share his simplicity in life.

After we came home, we started building a tiny house for our permanent residence. Our physical needs turned out to be tiny, and such a house requires radical choices and patterns that fit our value system and minimalistic ideals. A simple life, where you can't hide from yourself, the actual world around you, or your loved ones.

The Economy of Small-Scale

by Calum Creasey

Why small is beautiful and how vanlifers make money

Like many, when I first came across the film *The Powers of Ten* by Charles and Ray Eames I was blown away. In nine minutes the short video successfully lays bare the scale of the universe. A very daunting prospect. Seeing myself in the grand scheme of things for the first time made me feel very small. It sculpted the way in which I see the world to this day. When I was a young child our family of six spent a great deal of time in our camper van. Myself being the the youngest, and the only boy, it was often manic. But credit to my parents, for the most part we adored it. I think it is then that I began to question how big our homes really need to be.

It is true that dimensions dictate how we see the the world around us; the size of a leaf, the tree it is attached to, the field in which it stands and subsequently the sky that sits above it. Visualizing this scene is only possible with an innate understanding of the scale of these things. Live in a large city surrounded by tall buildings and you may feel small. Stand at the top of a mountain and the same might happen. Our size as human beings varies, but, in the grand scheme of things, by not very much. Strangely, though, the space we give ourselves to live varies massively. This sits on a far broader scale; a van, a house, a mansion, a tower block, a skyscraper. The relationship between the scale of our homes and how they make us feel may be counterintuitive to a westernized view of the world. One which champions scale as a mark of success, and maybe happiness.

It follows that a large house, with large rooms, requires a large amount of things to fill it. The heating bill is large and so is the maintenance bill. A large amount of effort on the part of the owner is required to pay for this large house. The energy this building consumes, the furniture that fills it and the time taken to pay for it require a large amount of effort and a great deal of time; something which is finite in all of our lives.

If we accept the above, then conversely very small houses require only a small proportion of this time and effort. This is to say that, if a small home can accommodate all that you require to feel comfortable, it requires less time and effort to reach the same destination, in terms of happiness, than it does the owner of the large house. This is the basis of the economy of small-scale, where happiness is the base currency and time and relative effort are valued differently than, let's say, a traditional Western model of economics.

Now let us present one of the most common vanlife-related questions you may ask: 'How do you make money?' The best way to answer this question is to set the scene, a very small scene. The average van is smaller than the average room in a newly built house in the UK. It takes far less effort to pay for a day, or a week or even a month, living in a van than it does to sustain a traditional Western-style house for the same period. This surely is one of the main motivating factors for the influx of people living in camper vans. From a personal economic standpoint smaller is far better. Combine this with a movement towards self-sustainability and the easy access of the digital world. What you have is an ever-increasing number of camper vans rolling around the world contributing to the economy of small-scale. A photographer, a jewellery maker, a writer, a designer, a consultant or a systems engineer. Working remotely, these people can make a key contribution to society whilst valuing time differently.

Spending little is the key to sustaining a life in a camper van and ways in which people make money vary massively. We have met those who work for six months and use that time to save for the six months of travelling that follow. Fruit picking or seasonal agricultural work are the choice of many. Travelling actors, musicians, craftspeople and labourers have been around for hundreds, maybe thousands, of years. Only now many choose vans as their means of transport. It is easy to see how arts, creativity and ingenuity go hand in hand with travel, thrive even, when people's minds are opened wide by new places and experiences.

Myself and Lauren have tried our hands at many ways of making a living. From temporary office jobs to volunteering in exchange for food and a free camp spot. We even had a good go at running a small business from the road. This started out well, but never reached a sustainable point and in many ways put too much pressure on our relationship. We love each other dearly but spending every moment together, with no boundaries between our work and our down time - that can become difficult. The one thing that we try to never forget is the importance of being flexible, and knowing when a job had run its course.

Much has been said of how the gig economy, that being temporary positions, contracts or job roles, supports a large number of people. It may be that in the 21st century we see economies increasingly underpinned by flexible working terms. The digital world provides the tools and exposure for many new ways of making a living. There are too many examples to count of people downsizing, selling their possessions and living in a vehicle. Opting for freedom to move, but also to choose how they exchange their time for money. When your living space is small and you spend far less, the demand to earn diminishes.

No matter how you pay for your van adventures, those pounds, or dollars or euros, can be made to go far, very far indeed. Be frugal and embrace the economy of small-scale. When the paycheck is happiness, who needs money anyway?

SPAIN

WORKSHOP

Chapter two

THE VEHICLES

If a Vehicle Could Choose ...

by Calum Creasey

An illustrated guide to our favourite converted vehicles

If a vehicle had a choice, I am certain it would want to be a camper van. Not a builder's van, a bus carrying screaming kids to school or a family estate car, but a camper van. I wonder if, during their previous lives, any of these vehicles had any notion of where they would end up. Did that painter or carpet fitter or taxi driver ever spare a thought for how the paint pots and the timber thrown into the back would one day be replaced with a cosy interior, lovingly crafted by their new owner? Did they ever catch a glimpse of the future – a couple asleep in the back, reading or making lunch? I like to think so. Next time you sit on a bus, have a little hope that one day it might become home to a whole family, a handmade kitchen in the place of the very seat you're sitting on.

I have seen a lot of old vehicles saved from the big scrapheap in the sky by people who can see the potential of even the most beat-up old vehicle. Vehicle design followed the trends of the era, with new models released every year. Some go on to enjoy a place in popular culture, while others fall out of memory, only to be picked up by later generations as their vehicle of choice.

MERCEDES 508D

A favourite of the Mercedes-Benz T2 models

Loved by many for their simplicity. The vehicle of choice for the likes of the Red Cross and emergency services across Europe. Today these vans are growing in value, due to their reliable engines and nostalgic styling.

VOLVO 240 ESTATE

Low-profile 1970s Swedish luxury

Estate cars offer the space for a mattress in the back, a longboard on the roof and as many passengers as you are brave enough to squeeze in. They also offer a relatively incognito way to travel for when the 'No camping' signs abound. The 240 estate is a bit of a boat off the road, but I love the styling and the bonnet that stretches out far further than you might expect.

MITSUBISHI L300

The bull bar says it all

Andrew Groves does a great job of explaining the significance of these small Japanese vans later in this book. I love them as they look like a people carrier on steroids. When bigger vans are left wanting by even the most basic of off-road terrain, these Delicas come into their own.

AMERICAN SCHOOL BUS

Hated by schoolkids, loved by the digital nomad

These things rack up huge mileage during their years of service. Deservedly so, they have gained a cult status and somewhat of a special place in Western popular culture. The school bus movie scene is still loved by Hollywood to this day – think *Speed*. For sale in the US for relatively low prices. You get a lot of vehicle for your money. With many different manufacturers they all seem to have the iconic yellow paint job. The vehicle of choice for modern nomad families across the US.

MERCEDES SPRINTER

The contemporary vanlife vehicle of choice

My first memory of these vans is driving them for the postal service here in the UK. They were big, fast and well used (abused). Chances are you have seen one flying down the motorway, covered in scrapes and dents. They were the courier van of choice from the early 2000s. The Sprinter has undergone something of a reinvention with its popularity as the base vehicle of choice, particularly in the US. For me they are a tad narrow, but I appreciate them all the same.

VOLKSWAGEN T25

The third generation of the Volkswagen Transporter introduced in 1979

The small, box-shaped, rear-engined van. In the US they have become known as 'Westys' after the well-known German converters Westfalia. Panel vans, window vans, high tops, pop tops, 4x4 syncro versions: there are many models to choose from. With a huge following and readily available parts, these vans are popular the world over. I think of them as a better-thought-out version of their older bay-window and split-screen ancestors, which is exactly what they are.

Compact Interior Design

by Lindsay Berresford

The basics of a moving living space and the fundamentals of compact interior design

With 69 (at the time of writing) bespoke camper-van conversions on Quirky Campers' books, we are yet to have two the same. Something tells me we never will. It is the smallness of the space that forces you to make choices, and those choices beautifully illustrate our different needs, tastes, priorities and skills. Not that you would know that from the endless identikit camper vans and motorhomes that have rolled off assembly lines for decades. But a revolution is taking place. People want to be involved in the design and building of their rolling home, and as is the case with regular full-size homes, as soon as the end user is involved, the quality and ingenuity of the result are in a different league.

There is interesting research to show that constraints actually enhance creativity. The small-living movement certainly seems to provide evidence of that. I've talked about choice and compromise, but the corollary to that are the incredible creators constantly challenging our ideas of what is possible in a space of that size. By designing things that fold away or serve more than one purpose you can create vastly more functionality in the same space.

I have been asked many times 'what makes the perfect camper van?' and all I can answer is 'whatever will make it perfect for you'. I know of a camper that was designed around the owner's desire for a waterfall shower and another that started with a pair of window shutters the owners fell in love with at a French flea market. Having said that, every would-be converter is well advised to think through the same basic questions to help them crystallize their vision. I have compiled contributions from the Quirky Campers community to bring you some philosophical musings and practical advice ...

What are you going to use your van for?

We learned the hard way that your needs change over time. When we first bought our van, Bella, we were a young couple looking for something to facilitate our lifestyle and adventures. Wild camping, weddings, festivals and trips to visit friends across Europe. Having a comfy bed and a cooker you didn't need to squat down to use felt like such luxuries that many other typical camper van features didn't even occur to us. It also didn't occur to us that Bella would still be with us eleven years and three children later ... This has meant a lot of retrofitting, including a fridge, a wood burner, two additional belted seats and an extra bed. Don't repeat our mistakes, and consider these questions in advance:

How many people will be using the van?

Design it for the number of people that will most often be using the van, then think about how to incorporate additional seats and beds for the occasions when they'll be more. Also consider whether that number is likely to grow - i.e. are you planning a family?

How sociable are you?

Not a judgement but a genuine usage question. We designed our van around the fact that we knew we would frequently be hosting friends and family and therefore seating six people round a table was essential. If you enjoy your own company or just prefer to keep your socializing outside the van, then it might make more sense to go for a fixed bed.

What kind of food do you like to eat?

Do you tend to cook or eat out? Do you eat meat and dairy? Is a cold beer at the end of the day the one thing you can't live without? Do you specialize in the art of the one-pot wonder or are you going to need three rings and an oven? These questions will help you to figure out the size of the fridge and cooker you need.

When do you plan to travel and for how long?

The weekend warrior and the full-time van dweller are likely to make very different choices about the size of van they go for and the amount and type of storage they incorporate. A summer traveller may be perfectly happy with a solar shower and a spade for their toileting needs whereas a winter adventurer may well prioritize an indoor toilet and shower.

How do you like to spend your time?

You may decide that space to store two folding loungers is of the utmost importance or build in a permanent bike garage. Wanda's owner below talks about how their choice of hobbies affected their design.

How we designed our van around our love of climbing - *Naomi Fiddes-Baron*

The most important thing about your camper van design is to consider why you wanted a camper van in the first place. We bought a van because of our passion for rock climbing and mountaineering and our wish to avoid 5am starts to get the best pitches at a climbing crag.

With a smaller van, getting the most storage without making the space feel claustrophobic or cluttered is a challenge; the trick is to think through precisely what you need, and design for that.

For instance, a drawer that doubles as a wetsuit wash for seaside days but fits a 70-litre rucksack full of a climbing rack and ice axes for inland adventures. Climbing bolts can be attached to the ceiling for hanging things to dry and can be transferred to the floor for strapping down the dog crate for travelling. There's a drawer that is measured specifically to accommodate two ropes and six pairs of climbing shoes.

Practicalities for every area have been thought of: a shelf above the hob is designed to hold prepped food and more space is added by a bespoke chopping board which fits over the sink, effectively doubling the available work surface area, combined with a corner top-loading fridge. Wanda imaginatively makes the best of available space.

Who is going to do the work?

One of the things that most excites me about what we do at Quirky Campers is promoting craftsmanship. I am a big promoter of using a van conversion as an opportunity to learn new skills, but also to support craftspeople.

It is worth doing a skills inventory – what skills do you and anyone else involved in the build already have? What would you like to learn? Don't be afraid to invest in paying someone else to do the bits that you can't or don't want to do – that is how to get the job done.

What craftsmanship means to us - *Anita Peggie*

Craftsmanship can be a scary word – it makes you think about precision, perfection even. I don't believe that's what craftsmanship is. When it comes to making a camper van, striving for perfection is a really bad idea! With a few basic skills and plenty of time to think about what you are doing, the carpentry needed to create a really beautiful van is within reach of most of us.

We love using recycled whisky-barrel oak in our builds. The imperfections in the wood add to the rustic charm we are trying to create. Creating as much as you can from reclaimed timber is the only way to go. It's really just a case of looking closely at what you have and seeing how you can use it to best effect.

There is a bit of a craftsman in everybody, and you can release that by letting go of your fear – don't think you need to be professionally trained – we're certainly not – just go for it!

What materials will you choose?

The choice of materials is what most clearly marks a quirky camper apart from a more traditional conversion. Out goes the rubber-edged melamine, plastic kitchen equipment and synthetic materials. In its place you will find reclaimed wood, traditional ironmongery, copper (lots of copper), wool and a host of other things, foraged and found. Start with what's easily available to you, perhaps you have a pile of pallets or some leftover tiles from a kitchen project: can you reuse the panelling in the van? Making use of what you have will save on costs but also inspire originality.

Materials - *Simon Newbury*

A few things I consider with materials. How nice will it look when I wake up in the morning. I like the contrast between different woods and I like the curves you can get out of wood. It's so easy to do and often covers a few discrepancies, whereas making panelling straight is harder to do well.

There are a few tools I have to have when I'm working: a palm belt sander, invaluable; a decent ratchet screwdriver; two good saws; a jigsaw; a couple of cordless drills; and a couple of G clamps.

I like doing more intricate design work in cedar as it's so fast to work with, almost weightless and surprisingly cheap if you buy rough cladding – it sands smooth in seconds. And remember, 8mm tongue & groove weighs only about 12% more than 5mm ply, some cedar in your mix or fabric will offset any extra weight by using T&G. Hard woods and thick wood are heavy, but can be useful for those small areas that get a kicking: worktop, kick boards.

I use a set of bathroom scales to weigh EVERYTHING that goes in the van and keep a record on a scrap piece of wood that's easily to hand so you always know how close you're getting to your payload limit.

If you think making something out of metal is a good way to go and you can't weld, you're never more than six feet away from a fabricator. I've had some cool solutions created from welded mild steel angle and saved weight, space and time.

tea India

How will you make it quirky and beautiful?

I'm fascinated by the question of who decided that all homes on wheels needed to be covered with grey carpet, that all motorhomes should only use a washed-out floral fabric for their upholstery (make that vinyl for VWs) and that sinks need to be made of beige plastic. For a long time, even self-builds seemed to be striving to re-create this look. But no longer. Aesthetics have finally come to camper vans, and artistry and creativity abound. There are so many ways to make your space homely, beautiful and a reflection of you as an individual. Here are just a few...

1. Upholstery – *see below*
2. Artistry – from painted murals to etchings
3. Splashbacks – reclaimed metal, handmade tiles, to name but a couple
4. Exterior decoration – be it paintwork or removable decals
5. Your 'stuff' – bought, found, made or reclaimed

Aesthetics - *Cat Sinnamon Large*

When designing the interior of your van, start with the colours. I would recommend not having any more than four or five colours. Using lighter colours will make it feel more spacious. You can still adorn it with bright cushions, quilts and beautiful items to make it cosy.

One element that ties everything together is the trim (auto upholstery, e.g. the seats, armrests, door cards, headliners, etc.) and other soft furnishings (e.g. cushion covers, curtains, rugs and bed linen). As a trimmer and a van owner, I feel that aesthetic bliss is achieved in the details. This can be very simple. A splash of colour that is consistently used throughout the van from the cushion piping to a painted kitchen drawer, the crockery to the fabric for curtains and bed linen. You'll be amazed how these small touches impact on the feel of the space.

When choosing your fabric, you will want to link back to your colour scheme as suggested above. You need to ensure a balance between durability, practicality and creativity. Vinyl and leather are both extremely practical materials; tough and wipe-clean, which is a big advantage if you have children and/or pets. Check out the detailed information fabric companies provide. The 'rub count' will let you know its suitability for your intended usage. Please remember that there are many factors that can affect fabrics' durability, including UV exposure, washing, dirt, flame-retardant treatments and pets.

What can we conclude from these contributions? There is a camper van converter in all of us. There is no 'right' way to do it but so many people to learn from. As in life, don't attempt a second-rate version of someone else's idea, but create the very best version of your own.

Mercedes Vario 4x4

by Becky Gaskin

Case study 1

I'm Becky and I first met Ant about 11 years ago at a local skatepark. He is a BMXer, and although he's too modest to say, he is very talented on a bike. He's also a talented cabinetmaker and a very practical person who can put his hand to anything. He knows only too well that you don't become good at something because you're naturally good at it. It takes passion and persistence, but more importantly you must enjoy the process of seeing how far you can possibly go. I think we both feel this same way about travelling in a van. It's never been about the van, it's more about where it's capable of taking us and our new van is certainly up to a challenge.

When we first met we used to go on road trips in the back of his Vauxhall Astra Estate. My surfboard, his BMX, a blow-up mattress and a camping stove all somehow squashed into the back. It was far from luxurious and liveable but it opened up a whole new world of possibilities to seek more adventures chasing the surf and finding riding spots all over the country. We soon realized we needed more space so Ant invested in a VW T4 which he converted from a van into a camper. Our trips then extended to Europe and we spent a lot of time exploring the south of France and Spain. It wasn't until quite a few years later that we started thinking about the idea of a more liveable space. One decision led to another and we finally sold our beloved T4 and bought a 1996 Hymer camper van.

This was one of the best decisions we ever made. Ant had always loved Hymers because of their character and build quality, and ours was certainly put through its paces and tested to its limit when our travels started to become more and more adventurous. We soon realized that vanlife for us has never been about the destination ... It's about the adventure along the way, pushing our comfort zones and exploring the unfamiliar. It was inevitable that in time we would start to outgrow our 2WD van. The desire to explore where the tarmac road ends first started in Morocco, where we navigated our trusty Hymer through landslides, up mountainous roads and across snow melt. But it wasn't until we arrived in Iceland that we soon realized we needed to take the plunge and buy a 4WD van. The possibilities of exploration suddenly became endless and we started to talk about the idea of driving a vehicle around the world. The potential of pushing a vehicle and our comfort zones to far corners of the earth where you discover a place and its soul really excited us. But first we needed to find a vehicle capable of overland travel as we would need to deal with river crossings, carrying extra supplies, water and fuel. We started looking for a new project straight away and, as by fate, our perfect van soon came up for sale. A Mercedes Vario 4x4 medium-wheelbase panel van, now affectionately known as 'Big Red'.

Why did we choose a Mercedes Vario 4x4?

The Vario is one of the only vehicles that bridge the gap between truck and van. We both agreed the medium wheelbase was a comfortable size to live and travel in, giving us a larger living space without compromising the exit angle too much. Its size also allows good manoeuvrability; the 4WD gives us great possibilities off-road; and the strong chassis and large weight capacity, carrying up to 7.5 tonnes, also help with the strains of off-road driving while allowing us to load the vehicle with extra supplies.

Designing the layout and building our dream van

As with all overland travel, we plan to be away for prolonged periods of time so we both felt it was important for our van to feel like home. Most overland builds are made really well, but in our opinion the materials they use could be improved. As Ant is a cabinetmaker we wanted to use his knowledge and skills to build something well made, practical and beautiful. When designing the space we took a lot of inspiration from the van itself. We wanted to keep the edges square but soft and fought to keep the gentle curves of the van's character with the walls and ceiling. These curves were some of the most difficult areas to overcome in the build, but were well worth the fight. We also took inspiration from boatbuilders' use of materials and the flowing curves and

SMOKING AREA

solid rounded edges featured in boat interiors. We often referenced back to the Hymer's interior, paying particular attention to the features we thought worked well. We ended up basing a lot of proportion sizes for the cabinetry on the units from the Hymer and took inspiration from their use of strong but lightweight materials.

As we often travel to beautiful places and enjoy spending time in nature, we also wanted to bring a natural element to the build ... as if we were bringing the outside inside. Where possible we tried to use eco-friendly and natural materials, and this theme will run throughout the van down to the smallest details. All of our cups and plates are made from compostable bamboo and glass will replace plastic where possible.

Materials

As we like to spend time in the mountains for prolonged periods of time – snowboarding in the winter – we decided to insulate the van with Celotex as it has great insulation properties and already has its own moisture barrier. We cladded the walls in lightweight 6mm oak-veneered ply which we sprayed white to keep the area bright, and the floor is a lightweight but tough lino to keep it fully sealed and to help act as a moisture barrier. The cabinetry is made from a mix of walnut and sprayed white-oak veneered ply. These materials were chosen for being aesthetically pleasing but lightweight and strong. Our garage walls are made out of 15mm white melamine and the garage floor is made from non-slip phenolic birch ply, both materials being tough and waterproof. Finally we cladded the bathroom in white PVC, again for its waterproof and lightweight properties.

Energy and electronics

When looking for a truck we didn't want to buy anything with modern electrics so that when we encountered problems they should be able to be fixed easily in most parts of the world. However, on this part of the build we had to compromise. We soon realized that the 4x4 Mercedes Vario panel van was very rare to find, so when one came up for sale we had to take it. Our van was made in 2005 so the electrics aren't too complicated ... if they were an issue in the future we should be able to simplify them.

Our van runs on 24 volts and our living space runs on 12 volts. We have a sterling split charger which charges our 12V system when the engine is running. We also have electric hook-up which charges both 24V and 12V systems when connected to mains power. We have decided to use two 110ah lithium batteries because they are quick to charge, are long-lasting and are able to be drained down to 20 per cent without damaging them. We also plan to install over 300 watts of solar panels on the roof to give us free power off-grid.

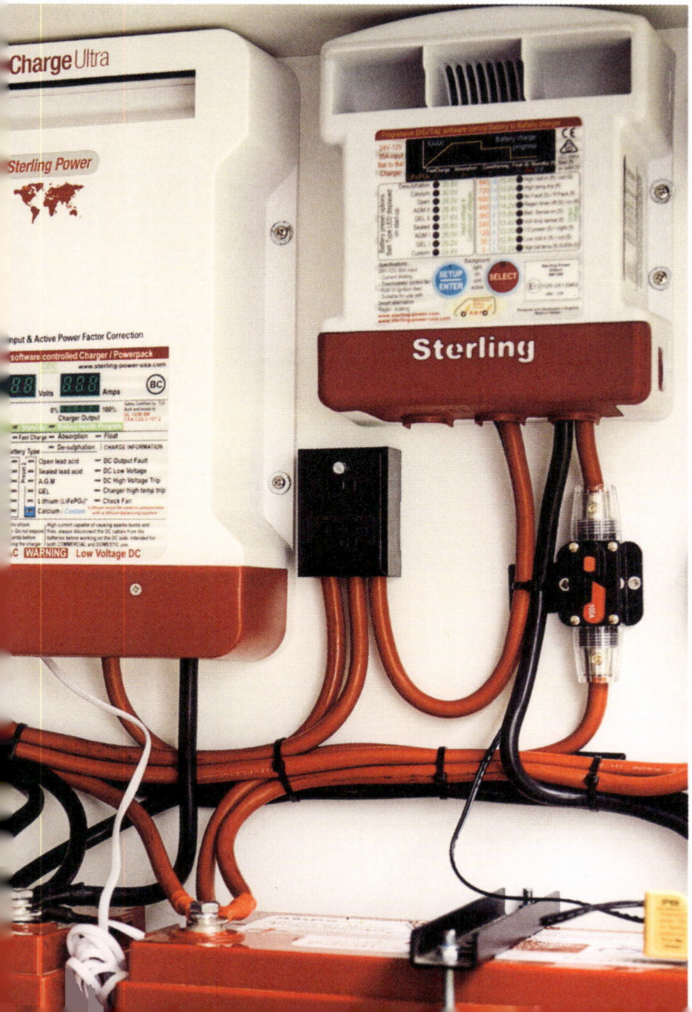
ChargeUltra
Sterling Power
Sterling
SETUP ENTER
SELECT
WARNING Low Voltage DC

Plumbing, heating and water

One of the most expensive items we purchased for our van was a Truma Combi boiler. This will be essential when camping in the mountains in winter, providing our van with heating and hot water. We ran heating ducts to different areas of the van, including the main living area, garage, front cab and bathroom to distribute the heat evenly throughout the van. We chose this particular boiler because it runs on diesel, which is widely available across the world. Connecting our boiler, shower and kitchen's water supply is a water tank carrying 125 litres. We positioned this tank under the seat in the centre of the vehicle to distribute the weight evenly throughout the van. We will also carry 40 litres of additional drinking water in jerrycans when we need to. A filling point was installed to the exterior of the van to top up fresh water and we have a small waste-water tank situated under the van.

Underneath the van we also installed a 20 litre Gasit LPG tank for cooking as we managed to source our other appliances in diesel or electric. We wanted a larger tank, but there wasn't a lot of space under the van due to all the tanks for the air brakes! LPG is easily sourced in most European countries, but isn't available everywhere so we will also install a gas point in the garage where we can hook up foreign bottles. We had previously used a cassette toilet but we both felt there must be a better solution. They felt out of date and made wild camping for long periods of time difficult as we would have to source a motorhome service point weekly to dispose of the waste. The mix of solids and liquids together also created sewage, which was horrible. We read a lot of reviews online about composting toilets and they seemed much cleaner and better for the environment, with no sewage or smells. They also require no plumbing and claim to last up to four weeks before they need emptying. We opted for the Airhead toilet and are yet to try it out, but the system looks much better than the cassette option.

The van is a few months from completion and we can't wait to start exploring further than we've ever been. We are really pleased with the outcome of the build and the space is such a pleasure to be inside. Although we have both poured our heart and soul into it, it is really Ant I have to thank for creating such a beautiful space for us to live and travel in. It really is a testament to his skill as a cabinetmaker and I'm so proud of him and what he has achieved.

VARIO
4x4

814 D
YN54 YFU

Volkswagen LT

by Clémence Polge

Case study 2

Some say the hardest part of any process is not the action itself, but making the decision to take action. Those people have probably never tried to convert a van on their own. Although, to be quite honest, deciding to have a go at vanlife was a fairly long process for us. It can be traced back to our vacation in Norway in 2015 and a road trip in Canada a year later.

Our tour of Norway lasted a little less than two weeks, during which we got on and off something like seven or eight planes. This, and the fact that the trip was so short, got us frustrated, as we were unable to really see the country like we wanted to. So for our following trip, we went the other way, rented a car, bought a mattress at IKEA, threw it in the back and drove from Vancouver to Calgary. That's when we realized two things: one, this was the way to travel, and two, this could be a sweet way to live! We had always wanted to spend some time abroad, but this road trip made us aware of one simple fact: we did not want to reproduce the same way of life, only in another country ... The idea of vanlife slowly made its way into our minds from then on. We discussed it at length, weighed the pros and cons. But at some point, it was either 'do or don't'. So we went for it.

And that is when the challenge became real, as we had to find a van that would fit our needs. Mainly, a van in which we could all stand (Thomas is 6'8"), as we were planning to live in it full-time for as long as we could. We also wanted a four-wheel drive, and we were on a budget ... So we looked; we had leads, most of them leading to disappointment. Until we found our big boy, a former vehicle from the Luxembourg police force, a beautiful Volkswagen LT40. Right next to our apartment when we contacted the owner. Perfect place, perfect timing! We didn't waste time, and after a short test drive, we shook hands on the sale: the dream was taking shape!

And that is when the challenge became super real. There was some major work to be done on the body of the van, which took over a month and the help of Thomas's dad (who would continue to be a major contributor in the conversion later) and a mechanic friend of his. We used this time to quit our jobs, empty our flat, move to the Pyrenees (where the conversion would take place) and wait for the Lieutenant (LT, it only made sense!). More than two months after we bought the van, the conversion was finally about to begin.

And that is when the challenge became super, super real – and pretty daunting, as neither of us had any real experience with handiwork at the time. While Clémence had used her interior architect and designer skills to draw the plans, the actual work was going to be a whole other adventure. Our team of three – thank the van god Thomas's dad helped us, he has all the tools and over 40 years of experience with them – featured all strong temperaments. Three people who like doing things their way, at their own pace. Which was never fast enough for us, obviously. As much as we love each other, this meant some pretty tough moments, to keep things polite. Especially as we realized that we had been extremely optimistic about the time we would need. Three months turned into six; our couple's strength was tested every day. But we held on.

As for the conversion itself, we learned as it went forward. And in all modesty, we did pretty well, given the circumstances. Some of the plywood panels, for example, are real pieces of art, sanded perfectly to fit the Lieutenant's curves. Sometimes, as we're chilling in the van at night, it is still hard to believe how messy it was at some points, how long it took to turn that dirty old thing (the former owner used to transport dirt bikes and spare parts in it) into a suitable living space. After more than six months living in it, we have yet to find a single thing that we would do differently.

Actually, the only real debate we ever had was about whether or not we should have running water in the van. Would we be able to keep the total weight of the van under 3.5 tons? More importantly, would having running water in the van fit our conception of this new way of life? In the end, we decided running water was not essential. And even after a long winter on the road, we still think we made the right call.

ER-259-ZL
@roammates

What we did indulge ourselves with, which was also a good call, is a dry toilet with a door. By dry toilet, we mean a bucket in a small space with an actual door. Pretty fancy! We could afford it in terms of space, and since toilets are not always easy to come by, whether you are in a city at night or in the wild during the cold season, it felt like a nice addition. And it turned out great!

All in all, we are very pleased with our work, and proud of what we have achieved given our total lack of experience. By all means, this was a long shot for us. But with dedication, and a bit (a lot!) of help here and there, we feel like we made a pretty cosy nest for ourselves.

The emotional attachment you feel to your house on wheels when you have built it yourself from an empty, dirty old van is quite strange. It is even hard to describe. Sometimes, the two of us discuss the possibility, or just even the idea, of selling our LT to find a more recent van with a better, more reliable engine. But even the simple thought of having someone else in there feels uncomfortable. Just thinking that someday our Lieutenant might not be able to take us on another adventure makes us sad. We usually cut these conversations very short, because we actually feel uneasy about that idea. That's how much we love our big boy!

All things considered, we are sure of one thing: turning a rusty army truck into our ideal rolling home and embracing the nomadic life was the right decision!

And if we chose to visit Europe as a start, it is also for our cat, Nel! We didn't want her to have to go through quarantine ...

Nel adapted very well to this new life, and the Lieutenant quickly became her home and her base camp when she goes off on a stroll in the wild ... She always knows where to run back to when there is danger! As for life in the van, we set up a nice sleeping spot for her in the form of a hammock ... But she always finds new spots for her naps, whether we are on the move or parked, hidden somewhere so she doesn't get disturbed or on high ground so she can see what is happening outside ...

Obviously, travelling with a cat implies some adjustments on a daily basis. We try to make the trip as nice for her as it is for us, and we adapt to her needs as much as we can. This means that we never stay out for long when it is too warm, that we always park in quiet areas with plenty of shade, and that we leave her with water and the windows or skylight open. Basically, Nel's comfort and tranquillity are always central to our decision-making process ... but it is so great to observe how she behaves in the wild and follows her instinct! Recently, she has even started eating out!

Delica Dreaming

by Andrew Groves

A venture into the wonderful world of Japanese vans

It's been almost twelve years since I lived in Japan, yet rarely a day goes by that I don't think of my time there. I spent one year living at the foot of the mountains in Hokkaido and another on the outskirts of Tokyo's bustling metropolis – both wildly different experiences yet indescribably formative. I was originally drawn to Japan by the aesthetic. As a graphic designer and illustrator, I drew endless joy and inspiration from the visual culture – the illustrated mascots and exotic typography, the sometimes uncomfortable mix of tradition and ultra-modern. I loved the garish neon signs juxtaposed against pure white snowy mountains and I loved the odd proportions of the minivans and cars – tiny, narrow and tall, like toy versions of real vehicles.

Although short, my time spent in Japan has managed to permeate nearly every facet of my life, even now. When I started to yearn for an adventure-worthy van a few years ago, I knew immediately that it could only be a Japanese vehicle that would satisfy my needs. I wanted something reliable; something I could fit surfboards, camping and outdoor gear in; something that was capable off-road; but most of all, I wanted something fun.

デリカ ドリーミング

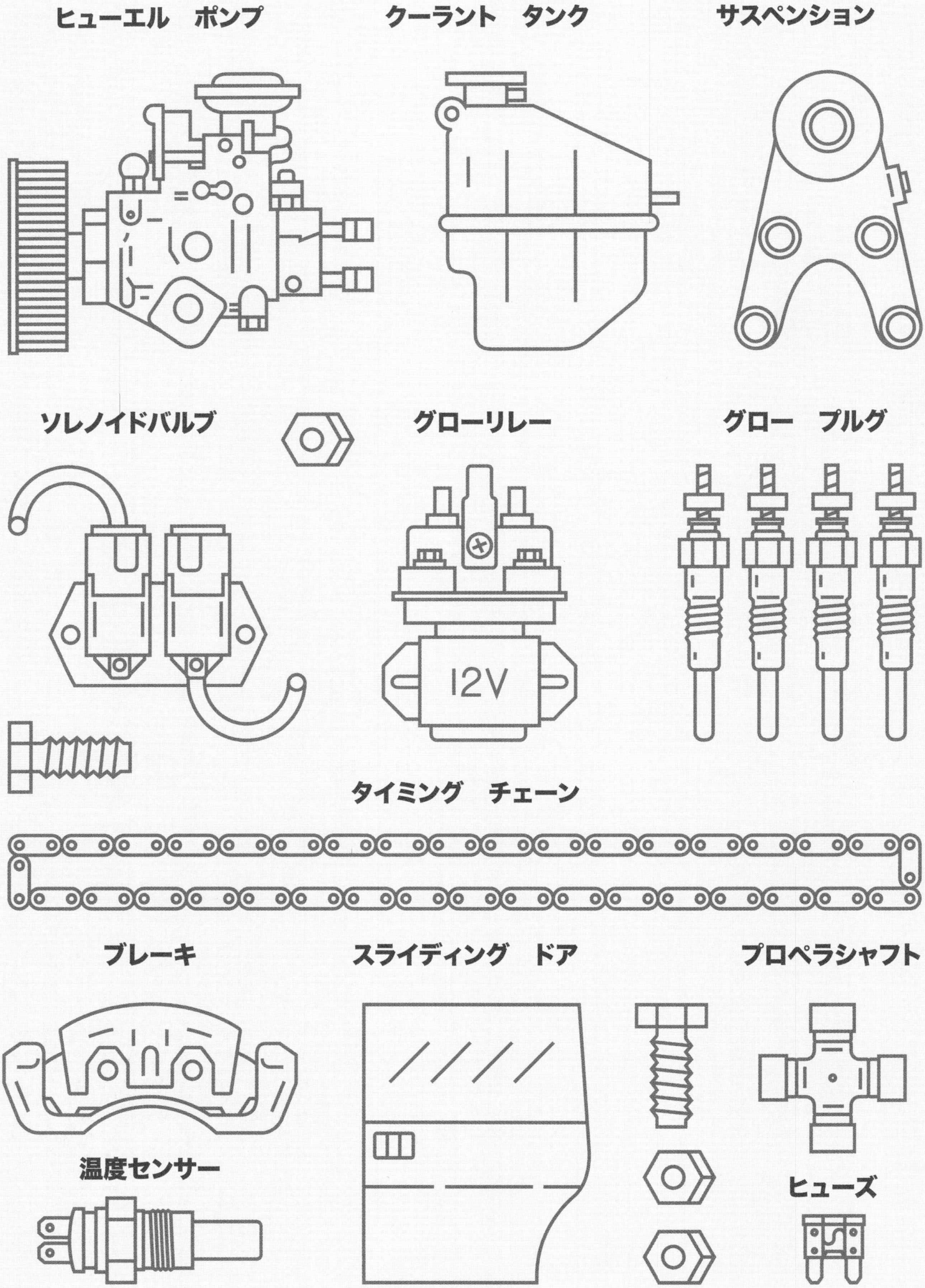
ヒューエル　ポンプ
クーラント　タンク
サスペンション
ソレノイドバルブ
グローリレー
12V
グロー　プルグ
タイミング　チェーン
ブレーキ
スライディング　ドア
プロペラシャフト
温度センサー
ヒューズ

A little cursory research soon sent me tumbling down an Internet rabbit hole into a world of weird and wonderful miniature wagons. The smallest class of road-legal vehicles you can get in Japan are called *kei jidosha*, which roughly means 'light automobile'. First produced in post-war Japan, *kei* cars are built to strict dimensions and engine sizes in order to qualify for lower tax and insurance and to meet emissions standards. *kei* cars have evolved to take on many forms, with campers, 4WD trucks, vans and even motorhomes all being squashed down to meet *kei* criteria, which goes a long way to explaining why Japanese cars look like they do.

Although the novelty appeal of a micro-camper was strong, I needed something bigger and a little more rugged. I don't remember exactly how I first discovered the Mitsubishi Delica, but once I had, I knew that this was exactly the kind of van I was looking for. Perhaps best described as a 4x4 MPV, visually the Delica reminded me of *kei* vans: tall, narrow, slightly squashed in appearance, oddly cute, yet menacing at the same time. High ground clearance, large wheels and chunky bullbars, side steps and ladders all suggested the versatility and off-road toughness I was seeking. Mitsubishi began production of the Delica in 1968 as a cargo van, but it's from 1982 onward, when they first introduced the 4WD option, that things got really interesting. Built onto a modified Mitsubishi Pajero chassis, the Delica is a capable off-road machine, equipped with low range and locking centre differential. With a few minor modifications you can take one almost anywhere. This was huge for me as I run workshops teaching outdoor and traditional forest skills, which sees me regularly having to haul tools, timber and camping gear up and down muddy forestry tracks in the woods near my home. I soon discovered that Toyota also made rugged 4WD versions of many of their passenger vans, the LiteAce, TownAce Wagon and HiAce Super Custom. Like the Delica, these were highly capable off-roaders yet large enough to carry eight or nine people in comfort. They had seats that could be swivelled, rotated, adjusted and folded flat into a full-sized sleeping platform. They even come equipped with sliding curtains as standard, making them ready for overnight adventures straight from the factory. Once you've been to or lived in Japan, it's easy to see why this kind of vehicle is common there; roughly 75 per cent of the landmass is mountainous and northern areas receive huge volumes of snow every winter.

For about four years after discovering that the perfect van for both my life and work did indeed exist, I dreamed of owning a Delica or 4WD Toyota. I signed up to receive alerts from Autotrader and eBay notifying me when they became available, even though I had no means of buying one. Money is tight as a self-employed doer of many different things. In those four years, I learned that Delicas are far more common in the UK, and cheaper than their Toyota cousins. I also learned that due to sharing an engine, chassis and various other components with the Mitsubishi Pajero, getting hold of spare parts would be easier for the Delica and so the Mitsubishi began to win my favour. My wife Emma and I would be unreasonably excited every time we passed a Delica in the wild. Purchasing one remained a dream, however, until finally, in 2017, an unexpected opportunity arose. Our second car, an old Daihatsu Terios that I used for hauling wood, driving to odd forestry jobs and local running around decided to die spectacularly. In desperate need of a replacement as we'd just had our son, Benji, we were given a small loan so we could replace it with a sensible car. Naturally we did the responsible thing, and promptly bought a rusty, beat-up 1996 2.8TD Mitsubishi Delica. Although less shiny and more bashed up than the Delica of our dreams, the dream was finally ours.

In the year that I've owned the Delica, at times the dream has been more of a nightmare. There has been a near-constant list of repairs and replacements, maintenance and modifications to complete: timing chain, fuel pump seal, 4WD vacuum solenoid, glow plug relay (twice), glow plugs, prop shaft, front-brake callipers, tyres, EGR valve, front-suspension ball joints, expansion tank, temperature sensor, welding, sliding door, rustproofing and underseal. In addition to the mechanical fixes, I've also insulated and ply-lined the floor, removed three of the rear seats and built a basic camper conversion. The latest addition is a second-hand roof-top tent and I think now, finally, I can say the van is ready for adventure.

Despite the problems, niggles and expense, we absolutely love the van. We love its obscure proportions, its sliding crystallite glass roof panels, its dash-mounted compass and inclinometer, its rugged charm. We love that all the interior warning stickers are in Japanese and that we can read them. We love that we opted for something different and that random people come to talk to us to find out more about the van. It's not perfect, and I doubt it will ever be truly 'finished', but every time I see the Delica parked in the drive, it makes me smile. Our van has transcended its ability to ferry people and things from one place to another and become something we are emotionally attached to. Something that reminds us of our time living in the mountains of Japan twelve years ago. Something that reminds us to always seek new experiences and adventure.

HIACE

1992 TOYOTA HIACE

1988 TOYOTA LITEACE 4WD

SKYLITE ROOF
4WD

4WD

1992 HONDA ACTY STREET

How to Build a Rolling Home

by Calum Creasey

A rough guide

Building the Rolling Home behind my dad's house with borrowed tools in my hands and a few sketches on scraps of paper, I would never have thought that it would lead me to this point. Yet here I am, pulling up the roller-shutter door to a small workshop in Cornwall, UK. If the first dream was to travel around Europe in a camper van, then the next had to be creating these vehicles for others to enjoy. In today's digital world, I needed to have those tools back in my hands.

Growing up and building things, working for my dad and learning how to handle timber and metal. Covered in dust, aching arms, design challenges to face and an end result to be proud of.

Onwards Adventure Vehicles is a company I set up with one of my best friends, Duncan. We share a love of camper vans, having spent many a cold night in tiny vans while searching for waves. As teenagers we skipped school and drove for hours only to be greeted with small waves and a blowing gale. What made it worth it was spending time in the van. The boiling kettle, the warm bed. The glow from the windows when you step out to watch the stars and the laughs we had on the long drives.

Including part of a build process in this book was a daunting prospect. What follows is an overview of turning an idea into a usable reality. Some of the choices are dictated by budget, some by design, and others are purely personal preference.

'Create a vehicle that makes you smile when you drive it and sleep in it'

This was the simple aim of this build project. I wanted to combine a base vehicle that I knew well with something unusual. Sure there may be better-suited models on paper and the Volkswagen T4 is far from original, but in a way this sets more of a challenge. To approach this build from a new perspective, hopefully paving the way for something very unique.

The concept

The aim was to illustrate the relation between the base vehicle and the living space. Sourcing these elements separately and successfully combining the two into a versatile camper van. Retaining a level of simplicity was key; the base vehicle would require very little modification. Admittedly in the past, and on other builds, I would have been happy to drill through steel panels, cut holes in the metal bodywork and modify the structure of a base vehicle, but with examples of this low-mileage and unmolested state becoming increasingly rare, there is a reluctance to modify the factory specification.

I have seen many builds of this type, along the lines of demountable camper shells that fit onto the flatbed of a pickup truck. I was also inspired by the 'Kaloha camper' built by Philipp Kentgens and the overland truck I visited in Milan, Italy.

By pure coincidence we happened on a miniature caravan for sale online. Manufactured in 1985 it would provide the perfect match to our 1990s styling of the Volkswagen. The dimensions are nearly perfect and with a total weight of 630 kg (including galvanized trailer), this would be the ideal base for our habitation unit.

Base vehicle

Stick with what you know. I know the Volkswagen T4, having owned one for over ten years. I am a child of the 1990s and I am a fan of the understated straight lines and somewhat subdued styling. Even the subtle introduction of a curve here and there hints at the approaching millennium and the introduction of a new age of vehicle design. To me this makes the T4 a product of a past era; they are very much my generation's split-screen camper. Somewhat of an ugly duckling.

I trawl online sales sites looking for vans more than I would like to admit. Always with an eye out for the rarer models. The thing worth noting about the T4 is the large number of them still on the road. Well looked after, they will go on for way over 200,000 miles. In fact our camper van has 240,000 miles on the clock. The sad thing is that finding a low-mileage example, in particular one that has not had its chassis welded or had any body panels replaced, can be extremely difficult. Even seemingly clean models can, on closer inspection, be uncloaked as very sorry-looking examples. Things to look out for are signs of body filler, mismatched paintwork and structural welding. Past MOT history (the statutory vehicle test here in the UK) can be a great help when deciphering the history of a vehicle. There is also the choice of engine to think about, since after all it is the beating heart of the build. The Transporter came in various versions from 1994 to 2005. Mostly diesel engines with a later addition of the VR6 petrol. I already own a 1.9 naturally aspirated (no turbo) engine and find it woefully underpowered. This base vehicle would need to be a 2.5tdi version, giving more power and comfort.

Back to the online search and every now and again a gem comes up. In this case a 2001 model with 40,000 genuine miles. A long-wheelbase flatbed Transporter with a single cab. The bodywork is in extremely good condition, having never been modified or repaired. The great thing about this particular van is that it had been used privately, and from inspection had never been driven in haste. The clutch feels fantastic and a full service history confirms that it has been well looked after. The cam belt and water pump were changed recently and receipts of this came with the sale. We also serviced the vehicle including draining and replacing the old engine oil and filters.

With a maximum payload of 1300 kg, this van would carry our habitation unit with no issues. The flatbed also provides the perfect surface on which to mount the structure of the pop-up caravan.

KP51 KXS
TDI

Habitation unit

The story of the Rapido pop-top caravan. Built in 1985 by French company Rapido, this caravan offered all the mod cons of its larger cousins but with more compact dimensions. This meant it could be towed by smaller cars. The overall height was kept to a minimum by the addition of a pop-up roof, reducing wind resistance and increasing fuel economy. Mounted on a single-axle twin-wheel trailer, the caravan already weighed very little (630 kg). We purchased the caravan second-hand, seemingly fully watertight but looking quite faded.

The tired interior offered little salvageable material. However, the factory layout proved to be a good use of space. The caravan has fully opening double-glazed windows on all sides, offering a large quantity of natural light. The pop-up roof would be the key to this build: pull on two latches and the spring-loaded hinges raise the roof in a split second, increasing the internal headroom by 40cm. This means that when mounted on the flatbed, the caravan's roof can be lowered when travelling and raised when parked, again reducing the overall height of the vehicle and minimizing additional wind resistance.

After dismantling the interior and checking the structural integrity of the shell, we removed the caravan from the galvanized trailer. Overall this reduced the weight to around 300kg. The perfect blank canvas for our build. The structure of the caravan had suffered damp from being stored for a long period of time. We took this opportunity to rebuild the lower part of the timber frame, reinforcing it wherever possible. The wheel arches, now redundant, were also removed and blanked off. I did this by removing the fibreglass mouldings from the lower quarter and replacing them with sheets of 'stucco' aluminium to match the rest of the outer skin. The pop-up roof mechanism was removed, before being thoroughly cleaned and resealed.

Shell & furniture

As with all conversions, minimizing weight would be key. Simple, sturdy unit carcasses built from birch plywood and faced with hand-built hardwood doors. This approach leaves us with a durable, mid-weight interior which really celebrates the timbers we used. Gone are the melamine and faced chipboard of the original interior.

In order to retain a light and airy space we opted for light tones and natural materials. The layout is similar to that of the original caravan with some alterations. What was the front of the caravan is now the rear of the vehicle. The profile of the shell meant that we had to reverse it when mounting on the chassis. Once the shell was emptied, we replaced the subfloor and reinsulated the walls and floor. The shell was bolted to the chassis using steel spreader plates and large galvanized bolts.

OFF

RAPIDO

Once this was completed we rebuilt the furniture, which now consists of:

- a small galley kitchen with overhead cupboards;
- the full-height corner cupboard making way for the base of the wood-burning stove;
- the two bench seats and central table that convert to the full-width bed;
- overhead cupboard providing ample storage.

Electrics

The addition of solar power to our other camper van was fantastic. It took a few years until we had the budget to add the system, but the first time we experienced the wonders of a cold beer, straight from the van, we knew we had cracked it. A well-fitted solar system allows you to keep your leisure batteries (separate from your vehicle start battery) topped up while drawing power for lights, fridges, heaters and charging outlets. Our system is based on a 12-volt circuit. All of the appliances we use draw a low amount of energy from the battery. This is key as it allows for sustainability. That is to say that we never use more energy than the solar panel can deliver to our batteries, even on grey and overcast days here in the UK.

We opted for an intelligent solar control unit. There is a wealth of information available online on makes and models. One thing I have found with building any camper van is that buying cheaper products can prove to be a false economy. If budget allows, opt for the more advanced systems that often provide better quality in the long term. Whatever form of batteries you choose – solid cell, lithium or wet acid batteries – they need to be well maintained. The lifespan of a battery can be ensured through intelligent charging. This means that rather than a large amount of charge being directed to the battery at any one time, an intelligent algorithm controls the charge based on the current state of the battery. Our electrical system itself is completely independent of the vehicle's system.

Remember to ensure that you use the correct-gauge wiring and connections when working with electricity. Reading up on the fundamentals before drawing up your wiring diagrams can save a lot of head-scratching. Safety is vital, so it is well worth having a qualified electrician check over all of your work.

We run two 100W solar panels through a solar controller and into a 115 amp-hour battery. From this we run fused circuits to each of our lights and appliances. The lights are all low-amp warm LEDs. Our chosen fridge is a 12V compression unit which draws around 3.5 amps at full power. We are happy to run this at its lowest setting. For charging of 240-volt appliances, we use a pure sine wave inverter. This is the most efficient way of converting 12 volts DC (direct current) to 240 volts AC (alternating current). This also provides protection for charging sensitive equipment such as smartphones and laptops.

Water

Our water system is very simple. The fresh (potable) water tank is housed underneath the caravan. It holds 70 litres and can be filled through a lockable inlet mounted on the side of the caravan. A 12mm flexible hose delivers this water to a pressure-controlled pump. We also fitted a pressure-regulating diaphragm to ensure smooth flow of water once the tap is opened. The pump senses the change in pressure and automatically switches on. The reverse happens once the tap is closed. Our drain outlet feeds to a smaller grey-water tank that is housed in one of our side lockers mounted underneath the chassis.

Heat

We have experience of diesel heaters, which are fantastic pieces of kit, but I have always looked with envy at vans with wood burners. While researching compact wood burners we stumbled upon Anevay Stoves, a company that handmakes stoves right here in Cornwall. We chose to fit their smallest model – the Shepherd – into the corner of the living space, leaving enough room around for safe operation. The flu exits the caravan through the roof and is protected by steel flashing. Remember to always fit a smoke and carbon monoxide alarm, and again have all of your fittings checked by a gas or heating technician

Equipment

One of the best aspects of this build is the versatility of the finished vehicle. We kept the aluminium fold-down sides of the flatbed, giving us space to store surfboards and place an outdoor stove when parked up. We modified the rear section of the flatbed with strengthening brackets, turning it into a space to store our bicycles. Underneath the chassis we added a storage locker on each side. As well as housing tools and gas bottles, there is also space for all manner of equipment such as wetsuits and windbreaks.

Build

The build was completed in our small workshop in Newlyn, Cornwall. It is a modest space with room for two vans at a stretch. With a three-metre-high roller-shutter door we were able to complete the whole build inside which makes the process a lot easier. After spending many years working on vans in the rain and on muddy driveways, I feel very lucky to have this workshop, especially when the winter swell starts hitting Newlyn.

There were a number of unforeseen difficulties, namely the damage caused by the ingress of dampness. This added a great deal of time to the rebuild of the caravan. This is often the way when working with older vehicles. Until you completely strip down a project, it is very hard to calculate how much time it will take you in total. The key thing is to persevere regardless, especially during moments of desperation. Take a moment, have a cup of tea and make a plan for how to tackle the new challenge – it will all be worth it in the end.

Once complete the camper van will go through a period of testing before being put up for sale. Either that or we will fall in love with it and find some way of keeping it. I think I prefer the latter.

RAPIDO

Left - re-building the timber frame.

Right top - bicycle carrier

Right bottom - kitchen unit and wood burning stove

The finished van

Chapter three

THE PEOPLE

Meet the Van Dwellers

by Calum Creasey

Archetypes of vanlife

When your home moves on wheels, your neighbours are forever changing. Meeting fellow van dwellers is one of the most rewarding aspects of vanlife. They might be just like you, or wildly different. See if you recognize any …

THE ADRENALINE JUNKY

Kitesurfing, mountain biking, climbing. You name it, she does it. Her van is 90% equipment storage, 10% living space. Seriously lean from hiking every trail she comes across. While the rest of us are searching for the slow lane, she is free solo climbing sheer rock faces in the American national parks. *Van of choice: Mitsubishi L300 4WD*

THE DIGITAL NOMAD

He runs a start-up, and as a result the van is more rolling office than rolling home. The latest in satellite technology keeps him connected anywhere on the planet, but failing that, he can pick up free Wi-Fi from a McDonalds a hundred miles away. Bouncing between LA and the Oregon coastline, he leads a reclusive lifestyle. *Van of choice: heavily modified Volkswagen Syncro T25.*

THE HIPSTERS

Never has a couple been so in love. They spend their winters in Portugal wearing very little. But who could blame them? Taking snaps, updating their social-media feeds and sipping on cold beers. Life is bliss. He is an aspiring photographer and the tripod is vital for taking the perfect 'just-woken-up' shot. The van is stacked with surfboards and even has an envy-inducing herb garden on the dashboard. *Van of choice: long-wheelbase Mercedes Sprinter.*

THE ECO WARRIOR

Her van interior is made from 100% recycled materials and is a wonder to behold. She spends her time volunteering on organic farms and promoting her type of 'van feminism'. Trees planted to date: 1,000,000 ... *Van of choice: beat-up old Ford Transit van.*

THE NEW-AGE HIPPIES

Their converted horsebox smells faintly of hemp and incense. Shared with five rescue dogs, all of which have a story of their own, it is dimly lit but warm and cosy. Despite the fact that it is slowly becoming a part of the environment and that it may have been a long time since it was deemed roadworthy, this vegetable-oil-burning diesel will go on chugging forever. Does it run on magic? Who knows ... V*an of choice: converted horsebox truck*.

THE GOLDEN OLDIES

These guys are smart. They took early retirement and spent the kids' inheritance travelling around Europe having the time of their lives. Their van of choice is a big white plastic motorhome with every mod con. Every single meal requires a full table set-up complete with chequered table cloth. They smile and wave when you pass them in the campsite, but don't get too close, as 'Ralph', their miniature Jack Russell, guards the van with delight. *Van of choice: coach-built motorhome.*

A-Z
Euromap

Slow 'n Steady Livin'

by Calum Creasey

Exploring a couple's approach to their relationship, jobs and creativity

Matt and Steph, tell us a little about yourselves. Who are you and how did you meet?

We are two creative souls who both have a passion for adventure. Steph is best described as a cosmic craftswoman, and her creative passions lie within illustration and photography. Matt is a salty seadog who spends most of his time in the ocean catching waves or teaching people how to catch them. He is also a professional photographer. Together we enjoy living a slow life, exploring nature and adventuring in our home on wheels.

When we first met, working at a surf shop, we would talk for hours about the open road and how incredible it would be to go on a road trip discovering new places and new cultures and sleeping in nature – and of course surfing every swell that passed. We made a plan, saved up, bought a van and the rest is history! We wanted to be more self-sufficient, to push our comfort zone and not be bound to one place. We both had a shared interest in 'alternative living' from a young age and that drew us together. Thousands of miles later, it has created the life we envisioned.

SLOWHAND STE
LIVIN'

Why did you opt for a van? How did your big blue Iveco come to be your home?

The first van we owned was in Australia. We had to cook outside, rain or shine. You couldn't stand up inside and we shared a single bed for a whole year while touring the coast. This tiny little home we created started our love affair with van dwelling and life on the road. It gave us a crash course in alternative living and the kind of freedom that tasted bloody beautiful!

When we returned to the UK, our first port of call was to purchase a new adventuremobile. This is when we met Ivy, our current van. Ivy is an eggshell-blue Iveco Daily 1996. The biggest selling point for us – apart from her having a kick-ass engine – was the space! She's a bit of a beast and perfect for a couple who live on wheels full-time. As well as having a fixed bed, we also have a garage space that is perfect for all our outdoor gear and surfboards. She was mostly 'fitted out' already with the original interior when we got her but we made quite a few modifications and personalized her to fit our needs. We did lots of DIY to make her our own. The biggest change was the fixed bed at the back – which was a must for us – as well as a table space on which to be creative, so we can use Ivy as an adventure wagon/moving creative studio. Steph had a vision of how she wanted it to look aesthetically and we tried to make those ideas come to life. We would say Ivy's a cosy bohemian surf shack all wrapped up in one!

Freedom machine, adventure vessel, rust bucket – whatever you want to call it. When your home has six wheels and surfboards on the roof, you can change your address at the turn of a key.

Tell us about your motivations. Living in a small space, as a newly married couple, must come with its challenges. Can you explain how you both support each other while being able to give one another space?

We would say that full-time tiny living could make or break any relationship. You get to know each other extremely fast; there is no space for hiding or not being yourself! We adore living in this space we created and built together. It's our sanctuary and a place for cultivating our creative passions personally and together. For us it's the perfect balance between exploring together and giving each other space allowing us time to pursue our own interests. We always come together in the evening to cook and eat together, which is something we also have a shared passion for.

For us, van living created a very intimate and close relationship. Disagreements are dealt with immediately and we usually end up laughing about it an hour later! As a result we have become excellent at communicating and knowing how the other feels, sometimes even without speaking.

60

We regularly have to work as a team, especially while on the road as van living comes with regular challenges – notably when your van is 22 years old! We've been in some tough and even scary situations in the past which we pulled through but where we had to support each other. Even with all the ups and downs, we wouldn't have it any other way! Overall, we're just happy living a simple life together.

What about your travels so far? A large part of your lifestyle is influenced by your shared love of surfing. How does this shape how you travel and the places you visit?

Of course we can't forget that living on wheels lets us move with the seasons and follow the swell along different coastlines. A big part of our journey consists of following the best swells and waves around Europe during the winter months, as well as dipping in and out of the mountains and inland landscapes. Travelling into the unknown on wheels makes us feel alive and it seems to be the only thing that can satisfy our constant hunger for adventure, our 'wanderlust'!

The majority of our travels are shaped in some way by the surf. We never stray too far from the coast and always keep an eye on the forecast. Being close to the ocean for us is a spiritual connection between Mother Nature and ourselves. It enriches our mind, body and soul, which is essential to our lives and happiness. It always makes us feel grounded and brings us so much joy personally and together, as well as being a treasure trove of inspiration creatively.

We love to revisit old favourite spots and boltholes, dropping in on friends along the way, while exploring new coastlines in search of quiet beaches and good waves. It has taken us far and wide over the years. Last winter we embarked on a surf trip to Western Sahara, joining forces with some travel companions, which was an unforgettable experience.

How do you balance your work and travel? You spend your summer working at a surf school in the UK and your winters on the road. Can you explain your roles, the workload, the flexibility? And how long have you been doing this for?

We split our year in two parts annually and have done so for the past five years. For around six months, the winters are spent on the road in our motorhome exploring. We spend the summers, usually from May to November, in the UK (still living in our motorhome but static on a friend's land), working the summer season.

We work together at a surf school in Cornwall, UK. Matt is the head surf instructor and Steph manages the bookings and coordinates the daily lessons. We both really enjoy working together. Life on the road has made us highly adaptable and able to work as a team happily. We also run our blog Slow 'n Steady Livin' throughout the winter and

summer. It incorporates both our creative outlets and is a place where we can share our photos and adventures from the road.

We usually work seven-day weeks so we are able to save as much cash as possible for the winter months. It's hard work and we are usually exhausted by November. The prospect of future travel always provides us with the motivation to work and save as much as possible. When the leaves start turning yellow in the UK, we know it is our time to pack up and head south to thaw out!

Would you say that this split works well for both of you? Is it a challenge to transition from travelling to being static and vice versa?

The transition from constantly being on the move to being static takes a while to get used to and we are always left with 'itchy feet' for a few weeks. However, we enjoy visiting our favourite haunts, catching up with friends and family, and recharging our creative batteries. It's always good to slow down and have a break from the uncertainty of the road, while having the knowledge that we will be off cruising and adventuring during the winter again.

As well as giving the van some much-needed maintenance before the annual MOT test and usually a lick of paint! For us, van dwelling is about creating roots in more than one place and enjoying every moment, no matter the location.

Splitting the year really benefits us creatively, as we have a winter of constant travel full of inspiration and working on creative projects together, then a summer where we can process and reflect on our work and make something of it.

Since you are on the road for long periods, how do you make your finances last? Is it down to rigid, well-thought-out budgeting, or do you take a frugal approach to spending?

In terms of budgeting, we've become adept at living cheaply (but also healthily, which is important to us). While on the road our only outgoings are food and fuel, plus general van maintenance. We usually have a weekly budget that we stick to when it comes to food. We like to live sustainably and also to eat a predominantly plant-based diet which helps keep costs down, as well as being frugal with water.

It's all relative as to what you think you need in life and what you choose to put your money towards. For example, we love being creative, exploring nature and surfing, and we find that living in a van lets us do this and gives us the freedom we are always seeking. Overall we have learnt that following what truly makes us happy is about making certain compromises: living with less, but experiencing more.

Digital Life

by Bee Roper

Theo and Bee on the digital aspect of vanlife

If you've ever typed in 'vanlife' on YouTube, chances are that one of the videos you watched was made by Theo and Bee. These guys are dedicated to their craft. They have racked up some serious views and subscribers. I don't think it would be untrue if I called them one of the best-known vanlife 'vloggers' in the world. When we finally crossed paths this year I was happy to find that they are just a regular down-to-earth couple. The World Wide Web has a funny old way of obscuring things; the vanlife movement is no different.

Why do the vanlife movement and the digital world go so well together?

The digital world can be accessed from anywhere with an online connection, which goes hand in hand with vanlife as you're generally only ever in one place for a limited time. The vanlife movement is now a flourishing scene, but it still captures people's interest, especially as it seems like such an ideal way to escape the norm and to try out a different lifestyle. Before social-media networks were around, these types of lifestyles were known but not mainstream, and the digital world has given the masses access to inspiration they would never have been able to find so easily not long ago. We've made friends with many people in the vanlife community through the digital world – which is amazing to think of, especially as it used to be taboo to meet people online; now some of our closest friendships grew through the Internet!

How has your own storytelling, particularly through film-making, allowed you to live a lifestyle of your own choosing?

One of the first things we did when we first set off to Europe back in 2014 in our VW T4 was to document our trip through Theo's camera and my words. We published our day-to-day experiences online, through our Tumblr and Instagram accounts, as a way to include our family and friends in our adventures but also to interact with others who were out there doing it too. Over the months this developed into film, as we thought it would add to our story if we could show what we saw through moving image as well. Using film as a way to document our day-to-day lives completely changed our dynamic, as it meant we were able to connect with people all over the world in a more impactful way; we've been told many times when meeting people who watch our videos that our viewers feel like they know us already and we are old friends of theirs. Our life has become our work and vice versa, which in turn keeps us moving and looking to do new things. In 2017 we spent many months travelling the country to meet up with other vanlifers who had turned their vans into their homes, creating short episodes for our YouTube channel about them and what they've done. Through film and the digital world we've made connections and shared stories with countless people, which is our number-one goal.

Are there any negative aspects to the relationship between the Internet and a search for a simpler life?

At times it feels almost contradictory to share our lives online, as it can open you up to a whole host of negativity and criticism. However, the positives far outweigh the negatives, especially when people reach out to us with stories of their own to share. Life can seem a lot simpler when you are disconnected from the Internet, and there have been times – like hiking the Kungsleden for 30 days – where we were completely cut off from the Internet for the entire duration. Life certainly feels a lot simpler when you don't have emails to reply to, images to upload or comments to respond to, but these are what we enjoy doing on a daily basis, so we feel the simple life and the Internet can go hand in hand. It's just up to you how much you let it control you.

How do you deal with the challenges of combining your passion for travel with your careers? Has your approach changed over the years you've been travelling in a van?

Neither of us had online careers before we began travelling, and at first they seemed completely alien to us. We never set out to merge travel and a career into one. However, we have been fortunate enough to have done that over the past few years. Our passion for travel allows us to continue to document our experiences online, which gives us the unique opportunity to work, live and travel all in one.

Bee writing the Indie Project's blog

Music in the Streets of Europe

by Sietske Riphagen

A short tale of friends making music while on the road

In the winter of 2017, while travelling in the south of Spain, we, Herman, Sietske and our dog Ferry, met Arnan and Anne who were also on the road, crossing Europe in their Volkswagen LT. Here was a couple with the same perspective on life and the same urge to travel. They even drove the same type of van. All of us had given up our secure lifestyle for a life full of adventure, all the while developing our talents and living by the day. We all experienced this meeting as predestined because we believe that God made our paths cross. We quickly felt that this could become an adventure for a longer period of time, and here we are, one year down the road! We are travelling together and busking in the streets to make money. None of us ever thought our journey would change like this. For us, this really is the beauty of having no plans. Our lives have become totally entwined.

A year ago, we would have never thought – although we dreamed about it – that we would be making money by busking. Anne and Arnan had already been busking during their travels. The first time we went out on the streets together was really exciting, but also a bit scary, because we hadn't prepared much. After our first experience we ended up busking every weekend. We soon found out that making music on the streets is much more than just playing nice and happy songs. Through music you can connect with people's hearts, which you sometimes can't do with words. Often, people come to us after performances to say that we made their day more beautiful, or they tell us what kind of difficult situation they are going through and that we encouraged them through our music. Also, for us, busking is more than just making money. Over time we have learned to set our priorities; life is about so much more than earning money. Life is about sharing, about caring for each other, and most of all about loving one another. How amazing to think that by busking in the streets we try to put this into practice and we get blessed in return, even financially.

We dream. We dream a lot. We talk about our dreams, but that's just the start of a new creative process. What we want to say is that you have to make a choice to go and make the step towards your dream. The good thing about travelling together is that we encourage one another in this creative process. Over the past months we have learned to bundle our talents more and more. Together we can do so much more. At the moment we are working on our own musical theatre performance. Working as a team is what we really love to do, looking for ways to bring out the best in each other. We are so curious about the plans God has in store for us and about how many roads we are going to travel together.

CHARTER
EMERGENCY EXIT
BRISTOL

The Wandering Bears

by Amy Barker

Family life in an old bus

We'd both had a taster of road life when we were younger. My family moved to California when I was a child, and while we were house hunting we lived in a tent for three months. It was an experience that always stayed with me. James also had experience of outdoor living. He left home at 18 and got a job in Robin Hood's Bay. Inspired by a family friend who lived in a bus, James lived in his VW Kombi on a nearby clifftop. He often talks of this time fondly and of how fit and healthy he felt, climbing the steep cliffs every day and the stillness of watching the sunsets and the changing sea throughout the year.

The main driving factor behind our decision to go full-time with bus living was motivated by slowing down our lives. In a way, it was less about the travel (although that is something we love too) and more about seeking simplicity. Living on our own terms, more frugally, intentionally and with a bigger value on our time. This fast became a huge priority to us after the most stressful period of our lives.

In 2012, we learnt of our daughter Holly's diagnosis of bilateral hip dysplasia. (Both of her hips were completely dislocated and not even in her sockets.) At the time she was five, and we were devastated. She required two long operations and had to wear a huge body cast for 15 weeks. What followed was a long and difficult recovery process, that took around two years of intense physiotherapy, to learn how to walk again. We were quite a carefree family before this time but this really shook us all to our core. It also meant that we spent most of our time indoors as Holly's wheelchair was difficult to manoeuvre when she was in a bulky cast. We became quite insular in a way. Soon something started to feel out of balance. We felt out of touch with the natural world.

Once Holly was mobile again we restarted her after-school activities. I was rushing around and barely seeing her and I thought, what is this craziness? It didn't suit us at all. It felt too soon. We wanted to get back the time we'd lost. We wanted to rediscover the natural world with her and to have some fun again as a family. James and I were both working stressful jobs at the time so were happy to take a break from them. We decided to just go for it and bought our bus Monty.

We wanted to build something comfortable that could sustain us long-term as a family. Something that felt like we weren't just surviving but thriving off-grid. The idea to buy and convert our bus couldn't really have come at a crazier time. James was working away from home a lot and would often be away for days at a time. Our son Forrest was only 14 weeks old and it was the middle of winter. The first major hurdle was finding somewhere secure to park the bus during the conversion process. Luckily we found a caravan storage yard that allowed us to store it and work on it.

This came with one massive drawback though: there was no access to power on site. So the plan was to install the massive solar rig first and to try and use the power generated from this for the rest of the build.

It soon became apparent that, even in the depths of winter, we were generating so much power it wasn't going to be an issue. Using mostly 18V cordless tools that were charged from the solar rig via an inverter, it became a seamless task. Soon James realized that he had done the entire build on solar, so he made the decision to carry on until the end of the build. The whole bus built on the power of the sun!

Overall the process took about 18 months. It took every ounce of strength we both had, as while James was building the bus or at work, I cared for the children. I don't think we've ever been so exhausted. I'm so proud that we never gave up and saw the project through as the rewards have been amazing.

James and I both feel healthier and more in touch with ourselves. I think so much of this is to do with the amount of time we have in nature, experiencing the changes of the natural world. Our first thunderstorm was so exciting. We all piled onto the bed and listened to the driving rain and rumbling thunder, watching out for flashes of lightning in the distance. We are taking time to appreciate the small things in life like cooking, walks and bike rides. But this lifestyle change doesn't happen overnight. We are still trying to discover what simplicity means for each of us.
It's all a process and it can't be rushed.

The sense of freedom is wonderful. There is a big part in both of us that doesn't like to feel tied down. Bus living provides the home comforts with an ever-changing view from our living room.

Because of Monty's size it can be a bit trickier to find places to park up. A lot of forward planning has to go into each journey. This can have its upside, though, because it means that we try to find places that we can stay for a little longer. This suits family life well as we can really explore an area rather than hop from place to place.

AMY'S BAKING YEAR
MOG
the Forgetful Cat

Hogwarts

We found home-educating a challenge to begin with. It's often what other parents ask me about when I tell them about our lifestyle. It took a while to get into the 'groove' of it but I soon realized that Holly was learning so many things from being outdoors and coming across so many opportunities every day. The world was her teacher, and isn't that the way it should be? We do interest-led learning – some call this 'unschooling'. I feel it's how we all naturally learn, by having an initial 'seed' of inspiration which leads to an interest and a want to 'grow' the knowledge in this area. By providing opportunities and suggesting ways to grow this 'seed' we've been able to cover topics in much greater detail and depth than she would experience in a traditional school environment. It's fun and gets us doing things we might not have done normally, as we all learn about the world together.

The kids have adapted to bus life really quickly, actually. We were worried it might be a difficult transition, having less personal space for Holly (now 10) and less floor space to play for Forrest (now two). These haven't been issues at all and they have really taken on the lifestyle with such enthusiasm, it's us grown-ups that have taken longer to adapt! The amount of outdoor time has really calmed Forrest down considerably. He has so much energy that he can really channel into outdoor play. Holly's confidence has grown massively. On a farm we stayed on recently the farmer's wife really took to Holly and included her in so many animal experiences, including caring for horses, sheep, alpacas, chickens and baby chicks. She even got to hand-rear a lamb, bottle-feeding it every day as its mother had no milk. She loved it!

The freedom to live how we choose on our own schedule, on our own terms, is why we love this life. It's not an easy road but it's wonderful all the same. The opportunities for us to learn and grow are plentiful. It feels like a real adventure. Watching the children blossom without 'hard' schedules in their life is also gorgeous to watch and I hope this continues to grow as they do.

It's lovely to see the kids bond more too. Holly and Forrest have a large age gap of eight years but they play together wonderfully. Although they have their moments I think bus living has brought them closer. When the kids are outside so much, plenty of dirt makes its way aboard but there's really no point in being too fussy about this. It's all part of the fun and being a small space it all cleans up pretty quickly. One thing that has really freed up so much time is not having the weight of so many possessions to look after. We had way too much stuff before and it had become a burden on our lives.

I feel glad we followed our intuition and gave life to our dreams. This lifestyle feels calmer, more authentic, and has allowed our true selves to be.

Good Vibes Only

by Brook James

Photographer Brook James on the trips made with his mates

We have spent a lot of time talking about the vehicles, but in truth it is the people that make this weird vanlife craze hit so deep. Although a few vanlifers may seek solitary roads with only themselves for company, the vast majority of us want to share in the good times with the people most dear to us. It's not just a chance to share the driving or the fuel bill or even the burden when it all goes pear-shaped. It is knowing that you all get to take a little bit of the trip back home with you, and will laugh about what happened in the weeks, months and years to come.

Brook James, a photographer from Melbourne, Australia, cherishes his trips with his group of mates.

You're rumbling down a forest track with your friends in front: what is going through your mind at that moment?

Usually what's going through my mind is, I hope they don't break down! Or if we are on a slippery muddy terrain, that they don't start sliding backwards. It can get pretty rough out there at times. But for the most part it's all safe fun and games. We take it pretty slow.

HELLA
CK·20·FO

After long tiring days of travel come the slow evenings. What does a group camp-out look, sound and smell like?

After a day of usually driving a few hours out to the bush where the tracks and camp spots are, we park up, eat some food and then hit the trails for the afternoon, and if all goes to plan, we are back for dinner around six or seven. A toasty fire is usually lit by someone who stays back at camp, so we arrive and start crafting our stew in the cast-iron pot which we let sit on the fire for an hour and a half, sometimes longer. We all huddle around the fire and eat our meal. Most of us are on the stew but others make homemade burgers or toasties. You have the crackling sounds of the fire alongside the calming sounds of usually a river or stream running next to our camp spot. It's a pretty relaxing set-up! We finish off the day/night with marshmallows and a few beers before we hit the sack and then do it all again the next day!

In any group there are always some characters. Who do you like to travel with most?

Ha, tough one. I wouldn't say I have one favourite person to travel with. I mean, obviously my girl and partner in crime of eight years, Brit, who is a champ. But outside of that, I am super happy if we get our usual crew to come. They are all good people and bring their own quirks to to the group. It's good vibes only and no d*ckheads.

Ode to the Solo Traveller

by Calum Creasey

Personal reflections on travelling alone, gender equality and empowerment

To travel by oneself is a challenge but the time that I have spent travelling in a van on my own has always been a valuable experience. The familiarity and sense of calmness that the van gave were empowering. Spending time with your own voice, inside your own head, is healthy. After all, how often do we spend time getting to know who we really are?

When alone, you become far more approachable than when in a group. As an outsider, the van with a single occupant is easier to approach than a large group of friends. I found that I make friends more easily, conversations flow and groups accept single travellers with ease. Despite this, I missed people. I craved not only those who were familiar, but also the knowledge that I was safe and secure. Some say that as men we are facing a so-called crisis of masculinity. And indeed, when I was younger it was difficult for me to accept that I found solo travel challenging. At first I believed that it was a test of being a man, that I should willingly be able to disappear into the distance, with little fuss. Proof of my rugged nature. A coming of age, a test. My version of leaving the tribe and spending time with the harsh realities of nature. As I grew older the importance of these early lessons became more apparent. Part growing up, part finding out who I was. What being a man meant, and what it did not have to mean.

I have met so many female van dwellers and enthusiasts that it is clear to me that the vanlife community is a place of equality, maybe even female dominance. Despite the seemingly macho things like oil and rust and spanners and engines. Despite what history books or tradition tend to show. To think that women are in any way incapable of being adventurers is very wrong. My three older sisters and mother have travelled far more extensively than me. That has inspired me, as a young man, more than any group of men heading off on a foolhardy expedition. This may be bold for me to say as a young man, yet we have discussed this at length in the *Rolling Home Journal* with many female travellers. But solo travel as a female comes with its own set of challenges.

In terms of gender equality, women still sadly face more stigma than men. The #MeToo movement and gender pay gaps in the West are all proof that there is still work to be done. But besides the cultural bias, there is nothing that separates a woman's ability to travel from a man's. The experience may differ, the reception in some countries may be different, but the human element is very much the same. In fact the most adventurous people I have ever met have been female. Women have a drive and an eye for storytelling that I think men sometimes lack. What solo female van travellers show us, besides breaking down our own cultural stereotypes, is that no matter who you are, a van can become home and take you to incredible places. This can be literal or metaphorical, physical or psychological. The fact that we may be more surprised to see a woman jump out of a van than a man says more about our failings and deep ingrained prejudices. It is travel that genuinely levels the playing field for all genders.

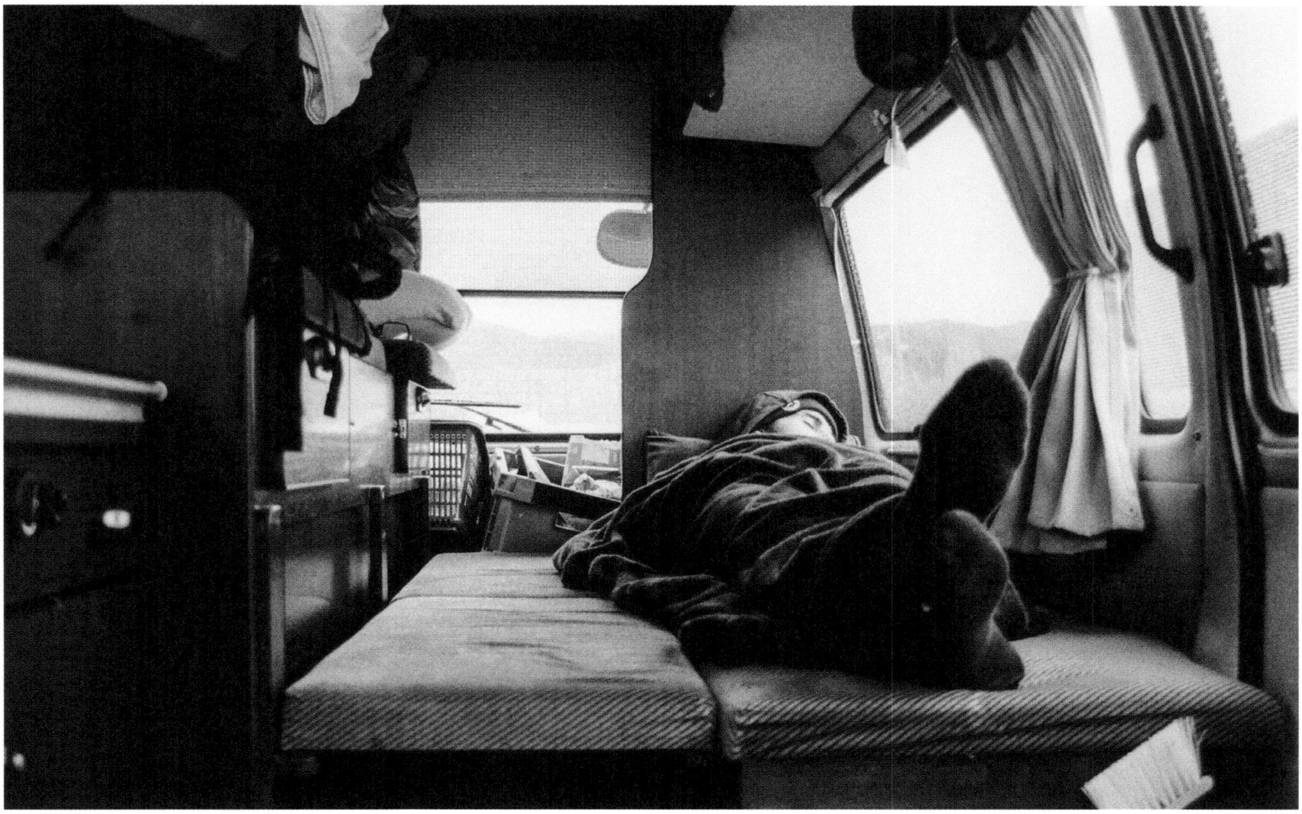

I THINK WE'RE LOST?

Chapter four

THE PLACES

Where Do We Go?

by Calum Creasey

Our favourite types of places

If I think of where we have been, the places that have been etched deep in our minds, I can feel a warm restlessness. A knowledge that those places are waiting for us at that very moment. Maybe another van is parked in that spot, and its occupants are discovering just how special it really is. Often it is the nondescript places, the ones that we stumble upon, that leave the deepest mark.

I recall forests bordering white sand beaches in southern Sweden. In early September, when we would wake up late with the low sun, feeling it slowly warm the side of the van. The Baltic Sea shedding its usual grey complexion in favour of a vivid blue. The archipelagos and small islands that made us wish we were towing a small boat behind the van or had space for kayaks on the roof. My mind strays to the rocky coves of Galicia in northern Spain, with beaches and waves all to ourselves. Or a blowing gale and rain for weeks on end. When all of the other travellers seem to be heading in the opposite direction. We were compelled there by the melancholy felt in the car parks of south-western France. When the summer swell disappears and other van dwellers are nursing hangovers, riding skateboards or playing music. Pouring over maps, trying to make the decision to head west or east. The first choice means the Pyrenees, the rugged Basque country that borders France and Spain. Afternoons eating pintos in San Sebastian with cold white wine down shaded alleyways. Mountain peaks that test the endurance of our little underpowered van. Second gear all the way to the top. The vineyards and the 'locals-only' spots. Surfing at sunset with the snow-capped mountains in the distance, a small Spanish town in the foreground.

Or we take the latter option and head for the Mediterranean. The Côte d'Azur, despite all the clichés and opulence, can still surprise you with hidden rocky coves and crystal-clear water. On to the Alps where the winter snow gives way to mountain-bike trails, the ski lifts taking walkers to the summit instead of snowboarders. Northern Italy, having our fill of Genoa and Milan before running back to the mountains and Lake Maggiore. Then we head north, over the passes and into Switzerland and Austria, or we continue east. To the Dalmatian coast, Greece and the gateway to Asia.

Whether, like us, you find yourself in Europe and have 50 countries to choose from, with a wealth of cultures, languages and food within easy reach. Or whether you are travelling through North America, a single land mass offering nearly every landscape imaginable. Maybe you are in Australia with its arid interior surrounded by thousands of miles of ever-changing coastline. Or you may find yourself in the depths of South America, where the rainforest gives way to high-altitude passes and some of the most remote places on Earth. How wonderful is it that these vehicles enable us to cover so many miles with relative ease. When the road stops they help us to find a beach or a desert, a valley or a walking trail. Rolling hills dotted with sheep and small rock walls. Mountain ranges with snowy peaks or vast inland lakes. We can roll off a ferry and be treated to a strange and exciting landscape. Or we can find just what we are looking for a few miles from home.

The art of van travel – and I would say there is an artistry to it – is never an exact science. Trying hard to find a perfect place to stay doesn't always work out. Sometimes you leave feeling disappointed. Frustrated that the map or the GPS or the recommendation from a fellow traveller didn't live up to expectations. Little do you know that the next destination has all of the little details you were looking for. The weather is just right, the mountain pass is open, the camp ground has a free pitch.

Where do we go? I guess the answer is any place we like, and some that we don't.

Vanhalla

In Norse mythology, Valhalla is the great hall that warriors go to after falling in battle. To eat and drink, to celebrate until the end of time. Besides this place of great renown, there is a lesser-known land, Vanhalla. Some say it is a fictional place, where camper vans and their inhabitants go to when they no longer travel. Rarely do you get to see such wide landscape laid out before you. An ever-changing tapestry of earth and vegetation. The effects of millions of years of erosion, shifting continents and ice ages. Winter, spring, summer and autumn existing together all at once. This map offers a glimpse into this place.

The Checklist

If you are in any doubt as to where to head for in a camper van, here are some of our favourite places: those we visited, those our friends visited, and a few we hope to visit one day.

Europe

Cornwall, United Kingdom

Our adopted home. Spring or autumn is the best time to visit. Avoid the summer crowds if possible. The small lanes get clogged up. It loses its slow pace and quaint feel from July through August. The small coves and sandy beaches can be breathtakingly beautiful. Free camping is at times difficult, but a bit of audacity can be well rewarded.

Outer Hebrides, Scotland

Take the ferry from the mainland and island-hop your way to the northern tip of Harris. Sheltered bays with white sand and crystal-clear water – often deserted, they make the best wild-camping spots.

Galicia, northern Spain

For us Galicia is reminiscent of the Cornish coastline. Hit it at the right time and Galicia feels remote - not cut off, but quiet in all the right ways. Good food, great waves and beaches. Enough space to park for free without worrying about locals.

West Coast, Ireland

It can be bleak and at times the wind can knock you off your feet. A rugged unforgiving coastline. Huge waves rolling on to the feet of ancient cliffs. Green fields, black peat and stone ruins. Western Ireland can be a wild place, especially in winter. But there is always a friendly pub and fire to retire to in the evenings. Spare a thought for the people who surf giants over hard-rock slabs – well worth a watch.

Landes, south-west France

Where many of us cut our vanlife teeth. In recent years the local authorities have clamped down on the scores of vans that descend here every summer, and maybe they are right to do so. But no matter how crowded the place gets between June and August, come September, this stretch of coastline, with its seemingly never-ending beach, pine forests and ever-changing sandbars, can be a hard place to leave.

Scandinavia

Öland, southern Sweden

A narrow island off the east coast of southern Sweden. Joined to the mainland by a single bridge. Mostly farmland, the northern tip is pine forests that run down to a rugged coastline. We spent a beautiful few days here in autumn 2013.

The Lofoten Islands, Norway

We have all seen the photos on social media and this may be a place that has fallen foul of too much popularity. We have heard stories of long queues lining up to take photos in certain spots. All of this fades into insignificance when you see the towering granite peaks rising sheer out of the North Sea. The small towns and villages occupy the low-lying land and islands. Think Northern Lights and a winter sun that doesn't set. Maybe even a freezing wave or two.

South America

Argentina, Chile and Bolivia

The geography is ruled by the mighty Andes mountain range, the longest in the world. Many ancient civilizations worshipped these heights. From flat plains thousands of feet up to deep dense rainforest. The altitude can take some getting used to. A spectacular part of the world that is home to some of the most colourful and mysterious cultures on Earth. If magic still exists on this planet, you can find it here.

North America

Joshua Tree, Yosemite & Death Valley, California

California has a lot to offer, so whether these three are its best isn't for us to decide. But it is a great place to start. Joshua Tree feels like the Wild West, only instead of cowboys you find campsites full of avid climbers. Death Valley is hot, as the name suggests. The camp grounds are a mix of retired couples in RVs and groups of young people in clapped-out vans that make for an eclectic mix. Yosemite is simply stunning, but it can get super-busy with buses full of tourists. Make sure you wake up early, climb the trails or walk through the meadows when the sun has not yet filled the valley. You can be forgiven for thinking you've stepped back in time a few thousand years.

Montana, Wyoming & Utah

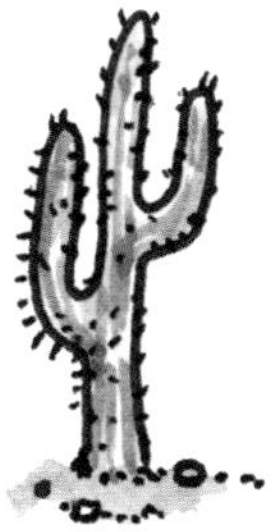

Think pioneers in horse-drawn carriages and wide-open grasslands that stretch to distant snow-capped peaks. Cowboys and timber farmsteads. The Rockies hold a certain magic – a Western frontier that still retains the promise of something new, if you are hardy enough to look for it.

Baja California, Mexico

A lot of people come here to escape. To remove themselves from society. In search of waves and a simpler way of life. It has a colourful reputation, in many ways for good reason. Anyone who has visited will tell you to take plenty of water, stock up on fruit and tinned food and be prepared to be cut off for days or weeks at a time. Oh, and to meet some interesting characters.

Africa

Morocco

This is many Europeans' first experience of Africa. Morocco is a melting pot of European, Arabic and North African cultures, architecture and cuisine. Part of a well-worn path and frequented by thousands of van dwellers each year. It is hot, colourful and beautifully vibrant. The Atlantic coastline is well known for its waves and free camp spots. Here is a place to absorb the culture. When the heat of the coast gets too much, seek out the Atlas mountains, or find peace and quiet in a traditional riad.

Meru National Park, Kenya

Think what you will of our impact on the world's wildlife, here you can see the most majestic of the Earth's creatures in their natural habitat. I was here in 2013 and I often saw overland vehicles and 4x4s with European number plates. If you have made it here in a camper van, then hats off to you.

Australia

South-western Australia

There is the modern backpacker's adage: 'Buy a van in Aus and travel up the coast until the engine blows up or you sell it'. This place is paradise for camper-van travel. The sheer scale of this coastline is remarkable. There is always more road to drive down, beaches to discover and camp grounds to frequent. Blue skies, even bluer water and white sand. If you're in a second-hand van, chances are it has done this route a fair few times.

Coles Bay, Tasmania

Freycinet National Park overlooks the Tasman Sea. A fantastic place to leave the van behind and take to some serious hiking.

India

Hampi, India

We have never been here, but a place can draw you in all the same. India does just that. Through the words of others we have visited. Rebecca Hawkes told us of this place in the *Rolling Home Journal*. She travelled there along the busy, dusty highways in a small van with four other people. Among the temples and the boulders, the colours and smells, she found something very special.

Canada

Tofino, Vancouver Island

Shayd Johnson's images will be enough to entice you to British Columbia. Tofino is a great place to set your compass for. Park alongside a saltwater inlet under the green forest canopy and set up camp.

Taffie and the Land of the Long White Cloud

by Alfie Conor Edwards

A vanlife story from New Zealand

From East London to the South Island of New Zealand, nearly 19,000 kilometres from home. A small plaque hidden inside the cabinetry of our van reminds Olivia and me of where this all started.

We met at Mudchute Farm in East London less than three years ago. I was a bicycle mechanic and Olivia a barista at a New Zealand-owned coffee roastery. Apparently cycling and coffee go hand in hand, and so did we. Having only known one another for six months we found ourselves boarding a plane for New Zealand together, our decision spurred on by personal accounts of friends and family. Our intention was simply to escape the panicked pace of London temporarily but, several visas later, the energy we once spent attempting to escape the crazed city we now spend engaging with and exploring the beautiful locations that surround us here in Nelson.

Leaving home is always tough. Friends, family and Florrie the dog were left behind. Most of us enjoy getting out of our vehicles and stepping into our houses. Olive and I feel the same behind the doors of our vehicle: with the turn of a key we can take our home wherever we like. It's become a halfway house that brings us closer to home in the UK, adorned with gifts from friends and an interior built decades ago in East London. At the same time the van lets us escape into the secluded scenery of New Zealand, taking us further away from where we came and closer to where we want to be.

Nelson Lakes is one of our most treasured little escapes. The day begins by loading the van full of snacks, far too many for our relatively short trip. I strap my bike on the rack and throw a helmet and a preassembled kitbag full of the essential spares and tools needed into the rear of the van while Olivia systematically stores her brew equipment, which consists of a hand grinder, an Aeropress, coffee scales, her beans of choice and, most importantly, her cup of the moment (which changes often but in case you were wondering is at present a Japanese Hasami porcelain mug), all of which go into their designated places.

We cruise out of Nelson making the obligatory stops for fuel, Olivia taking a 6oz flat white and Taffie guzzling 20 litres of premium. Thirty minutes later, phone reception is all but gone, a playlist of 90s R&B exits the speakers, and we cruise gently through rolling hillsides. Freshly sheared lambs fill the paddocks of the surrounding farms, and we spot billy goats, ponies, deer, various breeds of cattle and a lone horse that resembles Black Beauty. Like children on a school trip we wave at each one as we pass.

The farmlands thin out and dense forests fill our periphery. Commercial pine forests are supplanted with native beech, the hills turn upward, and it seems as if the van is going backwards. We crawl up to the highest point on our route, some 700 metres above sea level. The revs are high as is the oil temp. We spot a clearing to our left normally reserved for logging trucks but it's the weekend and the perfect place to let the old girl cool down, stretch our legs and get the kettle on. After all we deserve a cup of tea and have an abundance of snacks that we will do our very best to consume. During our timeout, a few vehicles pass us. The majority don't spot us, but of those that do, their expressions are either confused or concerned. I suppose a 35-year-old VW pulled over on the side of the road always gives an indication that help is required, but we are content.

The final leg of the journey into St Arnaud is short and thankfully flat. We drive straight on through St Arnaud itself, our objective being to get to the lakes. We pull up to the edge of Lake Rotoiti and quickly emerge from the van. With its clear flat waters and pebble-strewn edge, we scurry around searching for the best 'skimmers' we can find. I don't know what drives such an urge to want to battle the laws of physics but I hope it's one that never grows old.

Valais Canton, Swiss Alps, Switzerland

Van-ee-moon

by Hannah Stocks

An analog photo essay of Europe

Call us greedy, but we wanted a little bit of everything: the clear air of the mountains, biting glacial dips and steep altitudes which cleanse your lungs and leave you breathless. The endless surfing possibilities of beach breaks and river mouths, wild camping, salt-encrusted faces and the kind of sunsets which make you fall in love all over again. The peacefulness of the coastline together with a slice of action from the city, the hustle and bustle and, of course, good coffee. We wanted simple living for a month, day-to-day rituals, a slice of heaven on four wheels. We'd just got married; nothing seemed sweeter ...

Basque Country, Spain

Glacier lake, Swiss Alps, Switzerland

Cantabria, Spain

Moiry Glacier, Switzerland

West Galicia, Spain

Haute-Savoie region, French Alps, France

All the Mechanics in South America

by Xenia Kegel

A road trip from Germany to South America

We are Micha and Xeni. We are the kind of cheesy couple that spend every second together, making plans to save the planet and steal horses at night. We usually live in Heilbronn, a small town in the south-west of Germany. It's nice here, we have a lot, but as much as we love our home, we wanted to spread our wings and explore this world on our own.

So many times we have been asked the question, why go away? Our answer was always, so that we can come back and see the place we came from with new eyes. Coming back to where you started out from is not the same as never leaving. And how could we experience this trip better than in a home on wheels. It would give us the feeling of a home with the ability to explore new places and learn more about simple things. We wanted to leave the comfort zone of Europe and experience what life was about.

So, starting out from this simple idea in our heads, the trip became an increasingly real thing. A familiar story – we started by selling off all the stuff from home that we did not need. The less we had, the happier we felt. We learned that happiness is the consequence of personal effort. You fight for it, strive for it, insist upon it, and sometimes even drive around a continent looking for it. We wanted to make the most of our lifetime. From now on we would have all the time we were looking for – time to read new books, make bread over a fireplace, take long walks – and of course meet what seemed like all the mechanics in South America.

We talked about what vehicle to take so many times: 'Let's take a car', 'No, a Volkswagen T3', 'But Mercedes are stronger?', 'But this van looks nicer', 'How much money can we afford?' At last it was by pure chance that we found our Volkswagen LT 28. We were in Nuremberg, viewing a Mercedes van we had fallen in love with. But the inside was in such a horrible state. Right next to it there was the LT. Back then it was red, with a lot of rust and a really old-fashioned interior. But you know that feeling, when you enter a house – or in this case a really tiny one – and you feel like, yeah, this is it! Later we realized how unique this special vehicle really was. After we bought it we researched a lot about the LTs and I guess there are only a few with this kind of roof design in existence.

We proceeded to rip out the interior and rebuild it from scratch. Unfortunately we found mould and other creepy things - but for a van over 30 it's something you can expect to have to handle. Luckily we could upcycle a lot of material. We used wood from pallets and carpets from the company Micha worked at. We didn't think about what was most important at all. In fact we just wanted to create something that felt comfortable for us. Later, when we were on the road, we were able to modify the interior further to make it more practical. Also, the rust made us worry so we decided to give our home a new colour of paint – the stupidest idea in the end because after everything inside was nice and clean, it was really no fun trying not to mess it all up.

After we were ready with the conversion we shipped the van to South America. Our biggest motivation to travel was to meet different cultures. We learned some basic words of Spanish, but we didn't care at all. Filled with so much excitement we just jumped on the plane and didn't think about what came next. When we arrived in Bogotá, Colombia, everybody was so nice, so interested and welcoming. From then on we soaked up every single second like we were children. Everything was new, our brains were active and we realized that we could get pretty far with our few words of Spanish. We still recommend learning the language, though – very few people spoke English and even if we got surprisingly far in the beginning, it was also sad that we couldn't talk to more people the way we would in our own language.

Before we travelled to South America we had heard from many people that it was dangerous and that the streets could be bad places for travellers, that we should be careful with water and food and the wild animals. We quickly realized that this is just not the case. Of course we can only share our own experience. We followed some basic rules, at least in the beginning: don't drive at night (mostly because some streets have deep potholes); when shopping for food, park in the open; don't take too much money with you when in public. But nevertheless, we never felt unsafe or got into a bad situation.

Road conditions are another story. The further north you are in South America and the smaller the towns get, the worse the streets are. It can either be a fun experience or else you can be exhausted from the first minute of driving. We got the van stuck so many times – we got pulled out by horses and tractors or else just had to use our hands. The first time, we really panicked – but the deeper you sink, the more relaxed you become. The last times, we just cooked coffee and enjoyed the moment until someone came along to help. There was always someone.

We started in Bogotá and Balu, our van, arrived in the port of Cartagena. So we drove from all the way from the north of the continent to the south. Criss-crossing Colombia, from the Caribbean coast via the deep jungle into the mountains, the Volcano Nevado del Ruiz, over coffee farms in Quindio straight to Ecuador. Here we saw more breathtaking mountains, some of the highest on earth, including Chimborazo, where you can see the curvature of the Earth. Again we headed into the jungle and then to the other side of this beautiful country – the beach side. After a really funny hippie town called Vilcabamba, we headed to Peru and this was the first time we got a feel for the altitude. We stayed above 4,000 metres for most of the time and passed through the stunning Andes. One small town passed by an other, until we arrived in Caraz for Christmas, a nice town with a nice camp ground. We went to Lima, celebrated New Year's Eve and followed the beach to the Nazca Lines. Machu Picchu was one of our biggest and actually only goal we had planned in advance. Crossing Lake Titicaca we went to Bolivia, enjoyed the Salar de Uyuni and that was the first time when I, Xeni, got really sick. I walked into a cactus and got really high fever with diarrhoea.

Once I was well enough we left Bolivia and went to the wine region of Argentina. From San Salvador de Jujuy to Cordoba we marvelled at all the vineyards. From then on we crossed over between Chile and Argentina many times. This is not unusual because the countries are so close to one another, and crossing the border multiple times is the best way to explore. But it can also be exhausting because for some state reasons it is forbidden to bring food or any other animal products over the border. In the end we made it to the southernmost point on Earth that you can can access by car. Here we felt like the last people living on the planet. It was autumn in Tierra del Fuego and one of the best places we've ever been to.

We used to dream about escaping our ordinary life, but our lives were never ordinary. We had simply failed to notice how extraordinary it was. Likewise, we never imagined that home might be something we would miss. We are now back in our home town. We sold our good soulmate Balu the Van to the nicest couple in Santiago de Chile before returning to Germany. So for him the adventure goes on. We are now planning to travel through Europe soon. But this time by car with a rooftop tent. We really don't need much, as we learned on our journey through South America!

The Lucky Vanlife
HN LT 28H

Holiday from Where?

by Dane Faurschou

A photo essay of North America

My name is Dane Faurschou and I am a photographer, surfer, mountain-type guy from Byron Bay, Australia. I was living in Copenhagen for a few years, where I met my girlfriend, Sara, who has become my constant muse. We left Copenhagen together in February 2017 and have been living on the road ever since. When we started this trip we were not sure what would happen or if we would even like living in a van. The first few months were rough, especially being in Canada in winter, but now I honestly do not think we could travel any other way.

The photography aspect was something in particular that I wanted to pursue. Carrying a couple of bodies around, especially medium-format, is not always that practical and I find myself taking things out of my bag that I might actually need when what I do not actually need is two cameras. But there is some kind of urge there and for me getting rolls of film back from places that were pretty hard to reach a lot of the time is one of the most satisfying feelings. Sometimes I blow it completely, though, and then I hate myself.

Canada

I grew up in a small coastal town where the winter low is about 15 °C. I looked at the snow and envied the people taking photos there, thinking it was this magical wonderland with inspiration everywhere. I am not sure if that is true for every snowy climate, but it was definitely true for Canada. Our six weeks there in winter were harsh but I took photos and experienced things I never thought I would ever see or experience.

Squamish Chief

When I finally bought a digital camera a few years ago I felt like a sell-out, ha ha, so I went out and spent the rest of my money on a medium-format camera with the intention of hiking massive mountains with it in the snow. Maybe a little ambitious considering how much it weighs, but I have dragged it almost everywhere I have gone, including the third-highest peak in North America. When I bought the camera I pictured images like this – ominous, snowy, cold peaks with no one around. This was the first image I ever captured like that with this camera and it is still one of my favourites.

Ice Fields Parkway- *right*

There are a few images I shot that for me were our quintessential Canada experience, and this is one of them. It is difficult to capture the scale of the mountains and just how icy the road actually is. Each day you spend driving it seems to become more and more difficult. Not to mention it is not always easy to get out of the car when it is minus 15° to minus 20 °C. But I tried and we loved every second of it!

Mexico

Mexico has been filled with amazing places completely devoid of any kind of tourism. We had places like this to ourselves constantly. It can get a little uneasy at times camping alone, especially after a few experiences we had (think 10 to 15 men with machetes at night blocking a small road to a waterfall and trying to get us out of the car before I planted my foot and ploughed straight through them) but if you can calm yourself and accept that 99.9% of the time it's chill, then this will end up being a pretty familiar scene.

The Wave

Travelling constantly and shooting images of the same locations I had seen dozens of times on the net kind of stifled my creativity a little. You get caught up in the best lighting and best locations and it's pretty much a popularity contest. Even at places as mind-blowing as the wave. I wanted to start doing something a little different, to make people actually stop and look at the image. Being shot on film, it is a little more of a process than just creating it in Photoshop and I am putting together a series of images that hopefully slows down people's scrolling fingers just a little.

Private resort, Mexico

This, for me, is #vanlife. It is the reason we bought the van. Finding places like this travelling any other way is almost impossible. We don't have a big 4WD so we can't drive for days along beaches and through forests. This is about as deep as we ever really get. But finding super-fun longboard waves and turtles nesting in an area where there is nothing except a destroyed resort and spending a few days there with no one else around, surfing and drinking coconuts, is one of the perfect outcomes of this life for me.

Alabama Hills

Originally I shot this image as something to use as a story for Instagram. As it turns out it became one of my favourite images as far as photos of the van go. It was shot in the Alabama Hills as I was waiting for the sun to set to shoot something else. Outside of this shot it was kind of surreal, seeing something multiple times every single day (the background for most Macs is a scene from the Alabama Hills) and never really thinking about it and then just having it come to life before you.

Death Valley

This was a place I had actually wanted to shoot for years. I had seen photos of it but I only ever saw one that I felt did it justice and from that moment on I had been kind of obsessing over it. So when we were finally in the area my girlfriend and I camped as close as we could get, woke up an hour before sunrise and headed off to the spot to try and find the best angle. This might not have been it but every time I look at this image there is always so much going on.

Wells Grey

We had constant problems in Canada. I think we got bogged down five or six times. We got trapped into roads by small avalanches and also by trees. Armed only with a tow rope, snow chains and a shovel we managed to get ourselves out of every situation, except one, where we dug for about five hours, didn't move at all and at 10 at night a random car showed up and pulled us out. We did manage to move this tree, though, and everything was great, but Canada just taught us a little more patience and perseverance and every single problem was worth it in the end.

Documenting Vanlife in British Columbia

by Shayd Johnson

Photographer Shayd Johnson on the beauty of his Canadian paradise

Coastal British Columbia is a place ruled by the elements. Growing up on the edge of the Pacific, we were witness to its rugged beauty, from swells that have shaped the shoreline over centuries to old-growth rainforest that shelters and nourishes so much life. Even our most urban city, Vancouver, is only a stone's throw from the wilderness that defines our province. You can be driving through downtown, surrounded entirely by glass skyscrapers and catch a glimpse of the North Shore Mountains in their reflection on a clear day. Half an hour later, you might find yourself on one of these mountains, hiking along a glacier-fed river, or an hour still, and you've logged miles down a dusty logging road north of Squamish and ended up at a campsite with no one else around.

Because of its proximity to nature, I think most Vancouverites (and van dwellers who use the city as a home base) feel a greater sense of belonging to nature – and territorial over its use and management. Access to nearby backcountry areas is getting harder and harder (not just for vanlifers). A lot of these trails are managed by forestry and mining companies that put in gates and lock them at whim. But like many vanlifers out there, the people we've met in our part of the world are resourceful, and not just in finding the best spots to set up home. You don't have to go far to find vanlifers in Vancouver, though. There are a few special places only minutes from the city's downtown core. A rare gem in this beautiful seaside city that most vanlifers know about, a place where you can park in a large lot and find clean bathrooms, outdoor showers, and limited parking restrictions, all with an epic view of the city, is where I have spent most of my time photographing my subjects.

Unfortunately, in a city with a greater surrounding population of two and a half million people, where real-estate and rental prices have skyrocketed over the past five years, we've met people for whom vanlife is a necessity, not a lifestyle. Documenting vanlife culture in Vancouver is interesting in this way. It might be better than some alternatives, but it brings into question how fragile your sense of home and belonging can be. Long-time residents of Vancouver, suddenly evicted from their homes after 40 years of stable rental prices so a new condo development can be built, have had to resort to living in their vehicles. Students, too, who have decided to live out of their van to more comfortably afford their education. In Vancouver, vanlife is both a refuge and a harsh reminder of a reality for many vulnerable and marginalized people living in the city.

When I am out working on the series, I am often welcomed into people's home on wheels with open arms. These folks all seem to have something in common, whether it's just a sense of place or a true underground community that comes to light. They are excited to show off their creative alternative lifestyles, their DIY construction techniques or unique food creations. It is truly that, a small community on wheels.

FILIPPO BERIO
RIP CURL
RUDE GIRLS
WAECO
HO HO HOES IN DIFFERENT AREA CODES
K N I D
O E N

Naomi & Susan
1983 Mercedes ambulance

Two rad, adventurous, warm, approachable Dutch women on a journey with no end date and no final destination. Kind of like any other vanlifer, except theirs is one of the most unique and meticulously customized vans we've ever seen: a converted 1985 Mercedes German Army ambulance, standard-issue green with European license plates. They had their vehicle shipped from the Netherlands over to Halifax, drove across the country and were on their way south after a quick pit-stop in Vancouver.

Nick
Ford Transit

Nick was a great chance encounter. I wasn't intending to shoot that evening but I saw this cosy Ford Transit parked at the beach and couldn't resist stopping in to check it out. After just a few minutes I asked if I could run home to grab my camera and photograph him and his van, and he gladly accepted. When I returned, we got into some heavy conversations about aliens, atheism and philosophy before he told me that he actually taught philosophy to atheist children in an alternative school in Boston. Nick has been living on the road for a year and a half, travelling around North America playing music in his van (he is a Berkeley music graduate) and finding places to climb and explore. We dabbled in a bit of music in his mobile recording studio then watched Bigfoot videos on YouTube using a projector and a sheet that he had. This is the epitome of vanlife culture in my opinion.

ADVANCE49
AKAI
PROFESSIONAL

HYDRO
POWER

Chapter five

THE FUTURE

The Future of Travel

by Dan Crockett

What will vanlife and human travel look like in the future?

'When I see an adult on a bicycle, I have hope for the human race.' H.G. Wells

@insta_repeat is evidence of a widespread desire to capture an authentic and unique moment in nature. Countless curated posts show well-attired people on open roads and wooden bridges, in canoes, holding flowers and autumn leaves, pouring coffee, peeking out of tents, under waterfalls, on glaciers and spellbound by the Northern Lights. Each, in isolation, is a beautiful photograph. But they are presented in grids of twelve by separate photographers, four across and three up, each very nearly exactly the same. As modern technology blends with a global movement to seek freedom, we realize that we are anything but unique. Our travel experiences in the digital era come with their own baggage.

The days of Thoreau are firmly in the past. As the 'self-appointed inspector of snowstorms and rainstorms', he collected a visual record of the slow passage of time at Walden Pond. His connection to place was very different to that of the self-styled explorers of our age, but was the intention the same? While the nomads of the past understood the land completely, over the ages, as we have become more civilized, this has been lost. We have become severed and in some ways homeless. As Thomas Berry said, 'We are not talking to the river, we are not listening to the river. We have broken the great conversation. By breaking the conversation, we have shattered the universe.' James Agee hinted at the magnitude of what we try to capture on our mobile phones: 'There is no need to personify a river: it is much too literally alive in its own way, and like air and earth themselves is a creature more powerful, more basic, than any living thing the earth has borne.' While nomads of the past may have had some appreciation of this, social media distort the message. We compete for likes; nature is simply the vessel to achieve attention. No one could have quite foreseen this future in the present.

Each generation sees the present as reality. We guess at the future and look at the past with a mixture of scorn and nostalgia. Yet I grew up in a world without the Internet, mobile phones or personal computers. Consider that for a second. In under 40 years the whole landscape of the world has changed radically. When I was a child, communicating with relatives in Australia meant sending letters or perhaps even faxes. Sharing our experiences involved getting 35mm film printed and publishing the photographs. When I was born, a flight was a major undertaking and expense. The world's enhanced connectivity has completely changed the way we live. But where is this going? What is the future of travel? Digital technology, diesel-guzzling vans and plane tickets – the contemporary nomad's toolkit for freedom – are all contradictions in terms that don't really balance with living harmoniously on earth.

Furthermore, often the very things that allow us the freedom to roam make us feel more constrained than ever. Our experiences are mediated through a panoply of technologies, and we struggle to separate the real from the constructed. Even if we suppress it, we guess at the contradictions at the heart of our experience. The people who recognize their images on @insta_repeat are trying to relate to and connect with nature and their peers through the technology of their present. Ten years ago, it wouldn't have been possible to construct this account. Ten years from now, things will have moved on again. But how will all of this change? How will we travel in the future? Will be we able to enjoy a more nomadic life that is more sustainable than the planet-wrecking present?

Our entire modern civilization is based around a finite and uncertain supply of inexpensive crude oil. We rely on oil for everything. However, as Herbert Girardet says, 'if the growth in the use of cars is part of the development model we are promoting then we have no chance'. Cars and planes are killing our planet. About 15% of manmade carbon dioxide comes from vehicles. As Carl Jung said, 'our intellect has created a new world that dominates nature, and has populated it with monstrous machines'. What's worse is the effect on human health. Each year in the UK alone, 40,000 people die prematurely from diesel pollution. Yet in a contradictory turn, machines are now necessary for many people to get beyond city borders and to experience nature. It is well understood that what we see and experience, we care about and wish to protect. For the 75% of human beings that will live in cities by 2050, seeing nature is more important than ever. But it is hard for us to see it without killing it.

The last few hundred years have seen incredible leaps in technology that have created a population explosion. There are now seven billion of us, and meanwhile non-human biodiversity is in catastrophic decline. As Charles Eisenstein so clearly puts it, 'our civilization's millennia-long thrust to reach ever higher, ever deeper, to forge into new realms, to conquer every frontier. We have reached unimaginable heights indeed, but all around us we see the base of the tower crumbling.' The way we travel also robs us of feeling for the land.

David Abram points out that 'the unseen spirit of the land [is] mostly hidden to those who make the journey by car, since then all the senses other than sight are held apart from the sensuous earth, isolated within a capsule hurtling along the highway too fast for even the eyes to register most changes in the disposition of the visible.' If we contrast the modern nomad with someone like Peace Pilgrim, who walked an estimated 40,000 kilometres to try and bring peace to the world, it is clear that having a higher purpose is an excellent motivator. 'I shall remain a wanderer until mankind has learned the way of peace', Peace Pilgrim said, 'walking until I am given shelter and fasting until I am given food'. However, the way forward will not be on foot. Nor will it be on a bicycle.

How we build developing technology into our path, how we use it to better interact with the world around us, could become incredibly exciting. The future may well see better integration between what we are, the world we inhabit and how we interact with it. But whatever we use, whether we choose some futuristic van to do it, chasing freedom is and will remain a wonderful feeling. At its heart, this is an emotion we share with a thousand generations of travelling people from all over the world. It is a perennial part of being human. Right now this is exactly what the world needs. There is something in the human spirit that calls across time and unites every one of those who step outside of 'normal' experience. Remembering how lucky we are to have found this bend in the journey, to have glimpsed another way to experience our world, might just be the key to a smooth road ahead.

'The time has come to search the map for better possibilities, to strike out in new directions.' Bill McKibben

After Vanlife

by Sam Glazebrook

Continuing an alternative lifestyle after moving out of a van

At the start of a project, you can only imagine where it might take you. It might start with a drawing on a napkin, a conversation over a cup of tea, or some kind of dissatisfaction with the way things are. A drive to make them better – or maybe just different. All these things are certainly true for me.

When I started thinking about this cabin I was living full-time in a van, and that's all I had – a few drawings on a piece of paper and a conversation over a cup of tea with a close friend about renting some land on which to build a cabin. This was accompanied by the somewhat naive resolve of a complete novice that maybe, if I put my mind to it, I could do it.

One year and three months on, some things have certainly changed while others have certainly remained. I am still a head-scratching, barrel-scraping designer/builder. Learning with every project. I still have a shitty patchy beard and green, squinty, 'lined-before-my-years' eyes. But I am also different – as is this field in which I now reside. Still lined to the east with Turkish oak, brimming with the greenest grass which dances like lines of linen hung out to dry in the west wind (and still has the best sunset going on a clear night). But some of that which was once grass is now something different. Now there is a structure that resides here made from chestnut trees we felled and dragged through the mud. An idea that I drew on a napkin, scribbled into sketchbooks, then built using my two hands and with the help of a group of incredible friends and family.

It's always a gamble, when faced with an opportunity to rent land on which to build. There is always fear and trepidation, and it certainly isn't something that should be done hastily or without some real thought. For me personally, I knew I had to take that gamble.

I've lived here on this small farm for a number of years now, the first few of those years in my old van, Ferguson. A four-speed 1990 petrol LT35 with an aluminium Luton box on the back, found in the darkest depths of eBay and purchased for £1,000. He's got a small kitchen, a double bed, a small log burner and a dodgy sliding glass door which doesn't quite close (perfect for long, cold winters). All of which I installed with the help of a few close friends, for under £800, and which did me proud for some time.

In 2014, having just finished my studies, I'd recently returned from a trip to California to visit some family friends and surf some good point breaks. I felt called to return home – back to the UK and more specifically to Cornwall. Something about this place has always captured me. In spite of the long, cold and wet winters, there are pockets of magic here – where the sea shines emerald blue. Hues of pastel colours line the horizon at sunset, and again at dawn. Freezing but perfectly still mornings in the depths of winter offer up world-class waves and sprawling golden empty beaches for miles and miles. Long summer days stretching leisurely for 18 hours at a time. Late-night fires and long swims in secret coves. These are the moments in time that fill me with a true sense of belonging, and have convinced me to continue to reside in this small county and to call it my home.

The van was my access to this. Having just embarked upon my freelance career making films and photographs and playing music, I had little to no money to cover the standard expenses of your average human. Rent, council tax, bills, etc. Living in the van really opened up space and time for me to pursue the things I am most passionate about. There seems to be a mindset in our Western culture that has stuck in a lot of our minds to get a boring job in order to pay the expenses of the normalized way of life, having a nice big house, central heating, a new car. Are all of these things essential? Or more importantly, do they make us happy?

I'm a social creature. I love people. I believe in the power of community and friendship. It's essential for me. Living in my van would have been so much more of a struggle had I not had a good group of friends around me at the time. Especially through the winter when the nights are long and cold. I spent three years living in my van, and trust me, it wasn't all cosy Instagram posts and perfect beachside locations. Try sub-zero temps, damp bed sheets, borrowed sleeping bags and extra blankets, small gas fires from my dodgy cooker, smoke leaking through my unsealed flue, terrible MPG … I could go on.

After a year of ups and downs of living on the road, I came into contact with a local farm where I laid the van up for two years. This is where my dream was forged for a static place to call home. I knew I wanted to build it myself, and I knew I wanted to be here. So began a short but exciting conversation over a cup of tea, some drawings on countless pieces of paper, and a trip to the woods to fell some trees.

Come February 2018, the cabin was closer to being finished; I'd been sleeping in it more and more nights till in the early spring I got to the stage where I felt I was ready to let go and commit to selling the old boy and moving full-time into the cabin. It was an emotional experience, letting him go. I was stoked to move him on to a close friend, who I know will cherish and enjoy the experience of living in a van for a good while. It was still cold during the day, and freezing at night. So it was definitely my priority to get my heating sorted. As I'm sure many do, I find a lot of my bits and bobs in life on eBay. So I found a burner, and a good friend of mine whose father owns a building business hooked me up with some very reasonably priced, but fairly mismatched, flue. It still leaks a little in heavy rain – I'm working on that.

Having never built anything of any merit before this, I naturally encountered some pretty serious cock-ups. Some just small frustrations, constantly redoing notches and joins, getting angles wrong, snapping or rounding screws, or just having absolutely no idea how to make the thing watertight. The cock-up of most heavy consequence was my window framing. I found all my windows and doors either in dumps or through chatting to local people.

It was a warm but grey summer's day, a slight damp in the air. If you live in the UK you'll know what I mean. All was going to plan. Windows in, cladding 80% finished, doors getting hung. Finally I was seeing this building taking shape and starting to look like my drawings. The stoke was high. I decided it'd be a good idea to get my friend Ben to come and have a look. He's a site carpenter who lived a few hours north of me and was visiting for the weekend. To cut a long story short, he rendered my window sealing completely useless. I was gutted. I asked him what I should do. I very well knew the answer, but I asked him anyway. 'I'm sorry, mate, you're gonna have to take it all off and start again'. Ugh, that hurt. That feeling – you know the one – when your heart seems to fall through the bottom of your stomach. I thought I was doing so well, thought I'd finally started to figure out this building business after doing it for all of six months. How wrong I was. How naive. This conversation started a month-long process of unscrewing and crowbarring all of my beautiful waney-edged chestnut cladding, so that I could get to the stud walling where I had failed to seal my windows in effectively enough. Silicone is good, but not that good ...

I think the ups and downs of building your own place – or starting anything from scratch for that matter – could be likened to cycling through a range of mountains. I've done a little riding through the Alps and such places. The feelings are of high elation, blood, sweat, tears, swearing, laughing, singing, anxiety, optimism, beautiful views, pride, sometimes progressing with ease as though coasting down a smooth hill, encouraged onward by a light and warm breeze. Other times feeling as though you're battling a cruel and relentless headwind that will never allow you to reach your destination. Learning on the job, and working with friends with little to no experience, consistently present new sets of challenges each and every day. It's so much fun and so much work. I owe it all to these people in my life. Those who willingly came, expecting nothing, and gave so much to help me achieve a dream.

I honestly had no idea what the hell I was doing when I started, and I still feel as though I have so much to learn, and even now when I stand and look at the cabin, I find it hard to believe I actually built it. During those times of the winter weather setting in, with still so many jobs to do to get the thing watertight and insulated, I felt possessed by some unearthly determination. I knew it was going to get done if it was the last thing I did. There were also one or two people in particular who carried me through that time who remained positive, even through some of my darker moments. I think this is how we can know we are pursuing something worthy of our time. A true passion and a real conviction to keep going. I still have so many jobs to do, and my pace has certainly slowed somewhat, but over the last few months between travelling for work, I've built my small long-drop poop shack with most of the surplus timber, got my electrics sorted and started working on running water.

When I stop and think about it, which I often do, I can scarcely believe that it has actually happened. I think of all of the incredibly skilled craftsmen, joiners, boatbuilders and carpenters that I know and look up to who would've been able to create something far superior to this strange and wonky creation I see before me. I often wonder how I ended up in this position.

Don't we all so often do this? Compare ourselves to one another as if one person has more of a right to exist than the other? I was speaking recently to a new friend about the human disposition of self-awareness, and how it can be both a blessing and curse. As I write this I find myself wondering if I even should. If my words are even worthy of these pages. Regardless, here they find themselves, so I guess that's enough. I hope this little cabin in a field on a farm can represent something of this feeling to you as you read this and see the pictures; that as a human you are simply and intrinsically capable – that anything is possible if you have a vision and if you want it enough. I do believe that and have experienced it.

The last 18 months for me have been a new experience in so many ways. I've lost friends and loved ones to tragic illness, and with a heavy heart have stepped away from relationships in search of an inner stillness which continues to evade me. The one constant for me has been this small plot of land. I can't even call it my own, but it has become my home.

Index

Concept and design

Calum Creasey
Lauren Smith
stokedeversince.com
@therollinghome

Cover and end paper illustration

Katerina Kerouli

Copy-editing

Patrick Lennon

Texts

Amy Barker
Lindsay Berresford
Calum Creasey
Dan Crockett
Alfie Conor Edwards
Dane Faurschou
Becky Gaskin
Sam Glazebrook
Andrew Groves
Brook James
Shayd Johnson
Xenia Kegel
Clémence Polge
Sietske Riphagen
Bee Roper
Lauren Smith
Hannah Stocks
Mattias Wieles

Photo credits

Illustration credits

This book is
MARKED

MARKED is an initiative by Lannoo Publishers.
www.marked-books.com

JOIN THE MARKED COMMUNITY on

@booksbymarked

Or sign up for our MARKED newsletter with news about new and forthcoming publications on art, interior design, food & travel, photography and fashion, as well as exclusive offers and MARKED events, on www.marked-books.com

If you have any questions or comments about the material in this book, please do not hesitate to contact our editorial team: markedteam@lannoo.com

NUR 450/500 - D/2019/45/124
ISBN 9789401449779
www.lannoo.com

#AREYOUMARKED

THE ROLLING HOME

Man, woman or child. Spend time in a vehicle, any vehicle, travelling around this beautiful planet. Meeting the people, connect to the earth, making memories. Escape if you want to escape, find yourself if that's what you need to do. Leave work on a Friday and drive to the coast, drink wine, listen to music, fall asleep to the rain on the roof. Wake up alone and be excited at the prospect, or lie next to the one you love. Maybe the kids, who are sleeping up in the hightop roof, will wake you up too early. Maybe the promise of waves had your alarm ringing at 5am. No matter who you are - spend time in a camper van and, in doing so, embrace life to the fullest.

This book is dedicated to all of our friends and families who have supported our adventures over the years. A special thank you to everyone who has supported the Rolling Home by buying our previous book, copies of the journal and our products. This book was made possible by the contributions of stories, interviews, photos and illustrations made by so many incredible individuals, each with their own unique stories to tell.

To learn more about the Rolling Home and the *Rolling Home Journal* visit
www.stokedeversince.com - www.therollinghome.uk